The Segregation Struggle in Louisiana
1862-77

ROGER A. FISCHER

The Segregation Struggle
in Louisiana
1862-77

UNIVERSITY OF ILLINOIS PRESS
Urbana Chicago London

LIBRARY OF CONGRESS CATALOGING IN PUBLICATION DATA

Fischer, Roger A   1939–
    The segregation struggle in Louisiana, 1862–77.

    Bibliography: p.
        1. Negroes—Louisiana.   2.   Negroes—Segregation.
I. Title.
E185.93.L6F57   323.1'19'60730763   74–7230
ISBN 0–252–00394–2

To
Dale Somers
In memoriam

Contents

Preface

It has become fashionable among scholars to allude to the civil rights movement of the 1950s and 1960s as a "second reconstruction." Indeed, the parallels are inviting. In both periods coalitions of Negroes and sympathetic whites, aided enormously by friendly regimes in Washington, attempted to elevate the status of black people and expand their political and civil rights by waging war on the caste system in the South. Both times their efforts provoked the defiant opposition of a substantial majority of southern whites. Both reconstructions generated periods of conflict and confusion, fanaticism and violence, idealism and dedication.

Important differences, however, distinguish the "second reconstruction" from its ill-fated predecessor. The modern civil rights crusade has been essentially a Negro movement, spawned by black frustrations, molded by black leaders, sustained by the determined anger of the black masses. It has challenged discrimination on many fronts: at the polls and hiring windows, in public schools and places of public accommodation. In contrast, the reconstruction that followed the Civil War was rather fragile and patently superficial. It owed its precarious existence to the Radical Republican regime in Washington, a momentary idealism in the North, and an occupational army in the South. It was a white movement at every level of leadership. A creature of politics, it concentrated upon the ballot box, limited economic considerations to hazy visions of "forty acres and a mule," and for the most part ignored the volatile matter of "social equality" altogether. Lacking the grass-roots power and comprehensive focus of its modern reincarnation, the first reconstruction predestined itself to the limbo of history's lost causes.

In one southern state, however, the first reconstruction was much more than a struggle between Republicans and Democrats for the plums of political office. In Louisiana the decade of Radical rule after 1867 encompassed something of a "black power" movement in miniature, including the most thoroughgoing attempt to eradicate the system of racial segregation engendered in the South until the 1950s.

Reconstruction pursued a unique path in Louisiana primarily because of the peculiar nature of the Republican coalition in the state. There is little evidence to suggest that the white Radical leaders who came to Louisiana were more virtuous or egalitarian than their counterparts in other southern states. To the contrary, many of them were thoroughly unprincipled opportunists who mouthed libertarian platitudes while they lined their pockets. With a few outstanding exceptions the Louisiana "carpetbaggers" had neither the idealism nor the ability to lead a racial revolution, but they never dominated the Radical alliance in the state to the extent that white politicians did elsewhere in the South.

Negroes exerted an appreciable influence on the Louisiana Radical coalition. Due to the provisions of the First Reconstruction Act and the missionary mathematics of the Republican registrars who implemented it, black voters constituted a comfortable majority at the polls. Their ranks contained a generous number of proud, intelligent, assertive leaders, many of them products of the remarkable free Negro community in antebellum New Orleans. Born to freedom, these aristocratic *gens de couleur* saw the collapse of the Confederacy as an ideal opportunity to destroy the caste system and, at long last, achieve full equality with the whites. They made excellent spokesmen for the thousands of former slaves who might have settled for considerably less. Negroes first and Republicans a distant second, these black leaders made sure that their white cohorts never forgot the source of Republican political power in Louisiana. Blacks occupied a substantial share of key positions in the party hierarchy, local offices, and seats in the legislature. They were able to exert a measurable degree of "input" into the party's decision-making process. The end result of this influence was a vigorous campaign against caste discrimination during the decade of Radical rule in the state. The most ambitious—surely the most controversial—phase of that crusade was a concerted attempt to eradicate the practice of racial segregation in the public schools and places of public accommodation of Louisiana.

Since this study has concentrated primarily on that endeavor, rather than attempting to provide a more general history of racial discrimination in nineteenth-century Louisiana, certain aspects of the segregation system have been given minimal attention or ignored altogether. The division of many Protestant congregations and whole denominations along racial lines after emancipation seems to have been prompted in large part by the black desire to worship in privacy, apart from the annoying control and relatively staid ceremonies of the whites. This may have constituted a segregation of sorts, but hardly the conventional ostracism imposed upon a subordinate group to symbolize its degradation. Fragmentary evidence suggests a similar pattern of black voluntarism in residential segregation during this period, at least in the city of New Orleans. Unfortunately, little is known about the genesis of the "darktowns" that began to develop after 1865 as adjuncts to many of the smaller cities and towns throughout the state. Despite its enormous significance, occupational segregation did not develop into an important issue among Louisiana Negroes during reconstruction, in part because their aristocratic spokesmen failed to equate economic opportunities with civil rights. Not many New Orleans *gens de couleur* would have embraced Booker T. Washington's dictum, "The opportunity to earn a dollar in a factory just now is worth infinitely more than the opportunity to spend a dollar in an opera-house."

If this study appears to dwell unduly upon the public schools and such public accommodations as streetcars, theatres, and taverns, it is because the Jim Crow features of these facilities produced the greatest black resentment, were expressly prohibited by state and federal law, and thus developed into natural sources of friction between the races. For similar reasons, considerably more attention has been devoted to developments in New Orleans than to events in the country parishes, although slightly less than half of the state's citizenry (and a distinct minority of its black population) resided in the city during the 1860s and 1870s. New Orleans was the only community in Louisiana with a black leadership elite capable of mounting a serious challenge to Jim Crow and a black rank and file sufficiently unterrified to support such an endeavor. It was the state capital, where the 1868 constitution was written and subsequent civil rights legislation was enacted. It was headquarters for federal military forces in the area. As a result, New Orleans was the only community in all Louisiana to experience a successful assault upon its segregated public schools and an attack of any kind against its segregated places of public accommodation. From beginning to end, the struggle over Jim Crow in post–Civil War Louisiana was waged almost exclusively within the borders of New Orleans.

Since this study was begun nearly nine years ago, I have been the beneficiary of many kindnesses and a generous measure of competent counsel. Professor Charles P. Roland, who supervised my doctoral dissertation on this subject at Tulane University, provided painstaking guidance on research and style without once attempting to stifle an ideological viewpoint sharply divergent from his own. Another mentor at Tulane, the late William R. Hogan, provided constant encouragement and sound advice throughout my doctoral studies. I am indebted to the gracious and highly competent personnel of the Howard-Tilton Library at Tulane and the Louisiana State University Archives, especially L.S.U. archivist V. L. Bedsole. For his tough-minded criticism and generosity in sharing the fruits of his own research I am grateful to my good friend, the late Dale Somers, to whom this volume is dedicated. I owe a very special debt to my wonderful wife Susan, who with the patience of a saint tolerated my interminable harangues and muffled the noise pollution generated by our two exuberant little boys.

The Segregation Struggle in Louisiana
1862-77

ONE

Antebellum Origins

The Louisiana legislators who enacted the 1890 law requiring separate railroad coaches for whites
and Negroes were not really revolutionaries. Their handiwork
may have enriched the semantics of segregation and endowed it
with a certain statutory legitimacy, but it did not create the system. Racial segregation was already very old in Louisiana when
the lawmakers wrote their separate-but-equal sophistry into the
legal code of the state. First practiced in an embryonic fashion
before Louisiana became a part of the United States, segregation
developed into a complex system of interracial behavior during
the half century before the Civil War.

Segregation was obviously limited in the country parishes during the antebellum period by the very nature of the master-slave
relationship. On the plantations and farms, a formal separation of
the races would have been not only impossible but unnecessary,
for slavery was in itself the ultimate segregator. Perfect plantation discipline called for nothing less than what Louisiana planter
Joseph A. S. Acklen described as "the most entire submission and
obedience . . . on the part of every negro."[1] In pursuit of that
ideal, the slaveholders developed a psychology of command designed to implant in the mind of every slave a sense of abject inferiority and utter helplessness. Masters and overseers made use

1. Joseph A. S. Acklen, "Rules in the Management of a Southern Estate
—II," *De Bow's Review*, XXII (Apr., 1857), p. 378.

of authoritarian demeanor, constant supervision, rigid work routines, and systematic distribution of punishments and rewards in their Orwellian efforts to produce the perfect slave, the childlike "Sambo."[2] The psychology did not always work well, but its overall success was remarkable. New Orleans physician Samuel A. Cartwright once marveled at "the facility with which a hundred, even two or three hundred, able-bodied and vigorous negroes are kept in subjection by one white man, who sleeps in perfect security among them, generally, in warm weather, with doors and windows open."[3]

The totalitarian nature of the master-slave relationship made any secondary reminders of white supremacy and Negro subservience altogether unnecessary. Racial segregation on the antebellum plantations would have been absurd. Because familiarity carried with it no possible inference of racial equality, the masters and their families often took part in many of the social activities of the slaves. They frequently attended plantation religious services, listening with heartfelt approval as the preachers exhorted their black audiences with such apt homilies as "Servants, obey your masters" and "Blessed are the meek." They were often honored guests at slave marriage ceremonies and banquets. As Ellen Betts, born and raised a slave in the Teche country, fondly recalled: "When the work slight, us black folks sure have the balls and dinners and such. We git all day to barbecue meat down on the bayou, and the white folks come down and eat 'longside the colored."[4]

Racial segregation did exist side by side with plantation slavery in the rural regions of antebellum Louisiana, but it developed

2. Kenneth M. Stampp, *The Peculiar Institution: Slavery in the Ante-Bellum South* (New York, 1956), pp. 141–91; Stanley M. Elkins, *Slavery: A Problem in American Institutional and Intellectual Life* (Chicago, 1959), pp. 81–139.
3. Samuel A. Cartwright, "Disease and Peculiarities of the Negro Race," *De Bow's Review*, XI (July, 1851), pp. 67–68.
4. Quoted in B. A. Botkin, ed., *Lay My Burden Down: A Folk History of Slavery* (Chicago, 1945), p. 128.

only in special situations where Negroes and whites might be brought together in public as strangers. Restaurants and saloons were strictly off limits to blacks, as were the chairs and barrels in general stores where white men gathered to talk away their idle hours. Inns and hotels excluded all Negroes except the personal attendants of white guests, a practice which survived even the Jim Crow edicts of a later era.

Steamboats imposed a color line of sorts on their black travelers. Frederick Law Olmsted, riding from New Orleans up into the Red River country aboard the *St. Charles* in 1853, noted that while the whites bedded down in their cabins or on deck cots, he saw the Negro passengers "lying asleep in all postures, upon the freight."[5] But steamboat segregation policies were not altogether inflexible, as prominent free Negro barber William Johnson discovered when he attempted to secure cabin accommodations for his wife on the *Maid of Arkansas* for a trip from Natchez to New Orleans. At first the captain refused, explaining, "It was a Rule on his Boat not to Let any Col persons have State Rooms on her." But Johnson persisted and the captain finally gave in, complaining to the barber that the policy was dictated by the "Prejudice of the Southern people, it was damned Foolish &c, and that he was doing a Buisness [*sic*] for other people and was Compelld to adopt those Rules."[6]

Steamboat segregation extended to mealtime as well. Olmsted noted that on the *St. Charles* the white passengers were served first, followed by the white officers and crew, then the free Negroes, and finally the slaves.[7] Historian Charles Gayarré related the story, perhaps apocryphal, of a prominent free Negro planter who met a white neighbor aboard a steamboat. When the noon

5. Frederick Law Olmsted, *A Journey through the Seaboard Slave States; with Remarks on their Economy* (New York, 1856), II, p. 265.
6. William R. Hogan and Edwin A. Davis, eds., *William Johnson's Natchez: The Ante-Bellum Diary of a Free Negro* (Baton Rouge, 1951), p. 391.
7. Olmsted, *Seaboard Slave States*, II, p. 266.

bell was sounded, the stewards set up a small table off in a corner for the Negro. Seeing this, the white neighbor asked him to join his party for the meal. The black planter allegedly responded, "I am very grateful for your kindness . . . and I would cheerfully accept your invitation, but my presence at your table, if acceptable to you, might be displeasing to others. Therefore, permit me to remain where I am."[8]

Many Protestant churches in the smaller towns and rural areas segregated their black worshippers, though practices varied considerably from congregation to congregation. The simplest and most frequently employed device was a gallery or section of pews in the rear of the church to which the slaves and free Negroes were restricted. Many Episcopal churches conducted separate services for Negroes, usually on Sunday evenings. Some Methodist churches did this, but more often they set up entirely separate "missions" for their black members supervised by the neighboring white clergymen. Many churches of the various denominations conducted separate Sunday schools for black children, and almost all congregations excluded Negroes from participation in the organizations and social activities which they sponsored.[9]

Limited to such unique situations as commercial travel and formal worship, racial segregation remained a secondary, almost superfluous, guardian of white supremacy in the rural regions of antebellum Louisiana. But it was rapidly developing into a complex, comprehensive system of public behavior during the same period in New Orleans, the only major city in the state. As sugar planter Samuel Walker observed in his diary after a visit to New Orleans: "Slavery is from its very nature eminently patriarchial

8. Quoted in Grace Elizabeth King, *New Orleans, the Place and the People* (New York, 1895), p. 346.

9. Hodding Carter and Betty W. Carter, *So Great a Good: A History of the Episcopal Church in Louisiana and of Christ Cathedral, 1905–1955* (Sewanee, 1955), pp. 107, 113; Robert Alan Cross, *A History of Southern Methodism in New Orleans* (New Orleans, 1931), pp. 16, 18; John Tyler Christian, *A History of the Baptists of Louisiana* (Shreveport, 1923), p. 139.

and altogether agricultural. It does not thrive with master or slave when transplanted to cities."[10]

Walker had discovered that the complexities of urban life were making a mockery of the personal dominance over race relationships that was working so successfully in the country. On the farms and plantations, where identities were unmistakable and the roles of master and slave so absolute, no amount of interracial contact or fraternization could possibly bridge the great chasm between Negroes and whites. But in a city like New Orleans, direct discipline was next to impossible. In that world of strangers, white supremacy and black subordination were neither automatic nor implicit. Such basic activities as dining, drinking, entertainment, and travel became formal and institutional with the evolution of restaurants, taverns, theatres, and public conveyances. In New Orleans, interracial contact was systematically limited or eliminated by the whites to preserve the distinctions of caste in a society where anonymity was a fact of life.

Any attempt to maintain personal control over the Negroes would have been doomed by the very nature of the city's white population, by far the most heterogeneous in the antebellum South. Already a great international seaport linking the commerce of the Mississippi River valley with the trade of the world, New Orleans continually played host to thousands of transients from every corner of the globe. Moreover, the city was a principal port of entry and settlement for European immigrants. Of the 144,601 white residents enumerated in the census figures of 1860, 64,621 were foreign-born, including 24,398 from Ireland, 19,752 from the German states, and 10,564 from France.[11] Altogether, these immigrants comprised almost 45 percent of the white element and more than 38 percent of the total population of 168,675. In addition, a sizeable number of American-born New

10. Samuel Walker, "The Diary of a Louisiana Planter, Elia Plantation," typescript, Tulane University Archives, p. 28.
11. U.S. Bureau of the Census, *Population of the United States in 1860; Compiled from the Original Returns of the Eighth Census* (Washington,

Orleanians had migrated to the city from the North.[12] These Yankees and Europeans, born and raised in societies where slavery did not exist, constituted within the white community a large bloc not particularly sympathetic to the peculiar institution.

If the white population of New Orleans exhibited characteristics quite unusual in the lower South, the Negro community in the city was even more unique. Slaves, numbering 23,448 in 1840 before the sharp population drop of the 1840s and 1850s, enjoyed conditions far different from those of their rural counterparts. Domestic servants were accorded many of the prestigious duties of household management, including marketing and other tasks which allowed them to roam the streets, as the New Orleans *Bee* complained to its readers in 1835, "at liberty to purchase what they please, and where they please, without the personal inspection of any member of the family."[13] Other bondsmen were used as longshoremen, draymen, carpenters, mechanics, and factory workers. Along with the free Negroes, they monopolized the produce business, operating stalls in the markets or plying their pushcarts through the streets.[14] The complexities of these occupations brought responsibilities and liberties unknown to plantation slaves.

The most independent of all New Orleans slaves were those whose labor was "hired out."[15] This system, designed to meet urban demands for a fluid labor supply within the bounds of slavery, allowed an employer to rent the services of another

1864), p. xxxii. A brief summary on each of these immigrant groups during this period is found in Robert C. Reinders, *End of an Era: New Orleans, 1850–1860* (New Orleans, 1964), pp. 17–20.

12. William W. Chenault and Robert C. Reinders, "The Northern-Born Community of New Orleans in the 1850s," *Journal of American History*, LI (Sept., 1964), p. 233.

13. New Orleans *Bee*, Oct. 13, 1835.

14. Werner A. Wegener, "Negro Slavery in New Orleans" (M.A. thesis, Tulane University, 1935), pp. 58–60; New Orleans *Bee*, Oct. 13, 1835.

15. The best description of this practice is found in Richard C. Wade, *Slavery in the Cities: The South, 1820–1860* (New York, 1964), pp. 58–65.

man's slave. In some cases, these hired-out Negroes saw nothing of their legal masters except to turn over a stipulated portion of their earnings periodically. Many of them rented their own dwellings and led lives virtually free from white authority. The New Orleans *Daily Picayune* was hardly exaggerating in 1859 when it bemoaned the freedom of the hired-out slaves to "engage in business on their own account, to live according to the suggestions of their fancy, to be idle or industrious, as the inclination for one or the other prevailed, provided only the monthly wages are regularly gained."[16] In some instances, all that separated these hired-out bondsmen from full independence was the largely academic matter of their legal status.

Contributing to the unique composition of antebellum New Orleans society was a community of free blacks that numbered nearly twenty thousand at its peak in 1840.[17] Unlike most free Negroes in the rural South, who lived at the mercy of suspicious whites, the New Orleans *gens de couleur* exercised a broad latitude of liberties. As a truly diverse group, their numbers contained mendicants and moneylenders, bootblacks and brokers, prostitutes and poets.[18] Separated from the slaves by their legal status and set apart from the whites by the color of their skin, the free Negroes of New Orleans added a third dimension to the complex racial structure of the city.

Slave and free Negro attitudes reflected the unusual scope of freedom they enjoyed. As one student of antebellum New Orleans society has observed, Negro behavior was "singularly free of that deference and circumspection which might have been

16. New Orleans *Daily Picayune*, Jan. 27, 1859.
17. Their numbers declined from 19,226 in 1840 to 10,689 in 1860, due primarily to emigration provoked by a series of repressive laws aimed at them during the 1840s and 1850s.
18. The best description of their attainments is found in Donald E. Everett, "Free Persons of Color in New Orleans, 1803–1865" (Ph.D. dissertation, Tulane University, 1952), pp. 203–25. For a less objective account, see Charles B. Roussevé, *The Negro in Louisiana: Aspects of His History and His Literature* (New Orleans, 1937), pp. 49–91.

expected in a slave community."[19] In 1806 the legislature of the Territory of Orleans, perhaps indulging in a little wishful thinking, adopted a statute prohibiting free Negroes and slaves from presuming themselves "equal to the white."[20] Seldom has a law been more universally disregarded. To judge from complaints in the newspapers, black insolence toward whites was commonplace, especially along the *banquettes* in front of the many coffeehouses and grogshops that catered illegally but openly to the Negro trade.[21] Mourning the decline of race discipline in 1859, the *Daily Picayune* lamented that the blacks "have become intemperate, disorderly, and have lost the respect which the servant should entertain for the master."[22]

In the crimes they committed as well as the attitudes they exhibited, New Orleans Negroes, free and slave alike, made a mockery of the simple, deferential "Sambo" stereotype. Petty pilferage was common in the city as elsewhere, but the more imaginative black thieves stole horses, picked pockets, swindled, embezzled, and executed daring armed robberies.[23] The more violence-prone blacks assaulted whites with pistols, knives, clubs, stones, barrel staves, brickbats, billiard cues, broken bottles, horsewhips, cold chisels, and water buckets.[24] In race instances slaves and free Negroes even defied the ulimate taboo of a white supremacist society by assaulting or raping white women and girls.[25] These attacks on person and property constantly reminded the

19. Joseph G. Tregle, Jr., "Early New Orleans Society: A Reappraisal," *Journal of Southern History,* XVIII (Feb., 1952), p. 33.

20. Quoted in Everett, "Free Persons of Color," p. 167.

21. New Orleans *Daily Picayune,* Dec. 24, 1849; Jan. 3, Feb. 3, 1850; Apr. 1, 1855; New Orleans *Bee,* July 2, 1836; June 22, 1855.

22. New Orleans *Daily Picayune,* Jan. 27, 1859.

23. New Orleans *Bee,* Sept. 30, Oct. 12, 1835; July 1, 1855; New Orleans *Daily Picayune,* Jan. 16, Mar. 1, 5, 1850; Jan. 14, 16, Feb. 13, 1855.

24. New Orleans *Bee,* Sept. 30, 1835; July 12, 1853; July 1, 1855; New Orleans *Daily Picayune,* Feb. 6, Mar. 1, 1850; Jan. 14, 16, Mar. 8, July 19, Aug. 10, Sept. 27, Nov. 3, 1855; July 13, 1858.

25. New Orleans *Daily Picayune,* Nov. 11, 1854; June 2, 3, 1855.

white New Orleanians that theirs was not a world in which they commanded and the blacks passively obeyed.

In short, white control over the Negro population was conspicuously ineffective in New Orleans. The direct, personal system of race discipline that worked so well on the plantations simply could not function in a large city made up of absentee masters, indifferent strangers, and unusually cosmopolitan free Negroes and slaves. As that system disintegrated, the burden of maintaining the social distinctions between the races fell increasingly to a visible color line, imposed first in the city's municipal facilities and places of public accommodation.

Theatres and public exhibitions were officially segregated by a city ordinance adopted on June 8, 1816, which forbade "any white person to occupy any of the places set apart for people of color; and the latter are likewise forbidden to occupy any of those reserved for white persons."[26] This edict, most likely Louisiana's first "Jim Crow" law, merely ratified a longstanding local management policy, for most exhibition halls and theatres had long segregated their audiences by allocating rear sections or upper galleries for black patrons. When Bernardo Coquet renovated his ballroom into the St. Philip Street Theatre in 1810, he included in his alterations the construction of a tier of "upper boxes for women of color."[27] These galleries soon became known in the vernacular as "nigger heavens," an expression that survived for nearly two centuries until the practice itself was finally abandoned.

26. John Calhoun, comp., *Digest of the Ordinances and Resolutions of the Second Municipality of New Orleans, in Force May 1, 1840* (New Orleans, 1840), p. 144; Perry S. Warfield, comp., *Digest of the Acts of the Legislature and Decisions of the Supreme Court of Louisiana Relative to the General Council of the City of New Orleans, Together with the Ordinances and Resolutions of the Former City Council, and the General Council of the City of New Orleans, in Force on the First of August, 1848* (New Orleans, 1848), p. 129.

27. Quoted in Henry A. Kmen, "The Music of New Orleans," in *The*

Of all such seating arrangements, the one that invited the most comment from visitors was the gallery for the free Negro aristocracy in the French Opera House, the city's most prestigious cultural attraction. Thomas Low Nichols, the English spiritualist and food-faddist, wrote of the segregated seating as a great triumph for the *gens de couleur*, describing their gallery as "the portion of the house devoted to ladies and gentlemen of colour . . . into which no common white trash was allowed to intrude."[28] Other observers, however, interpreted the implications of the arrangement quite differently. Sir Charles Lyell, the eminent English geologist, made reference to the economic and cultural attainments of the free Negro elite and denounced their ostracism to the upper tier as a "tyranny of caste."[29] The Hungarian travelers Ferencz and Theresa Pulszky reacted in a similar manner. Fascinated by the paradox inherent in the social position occupied by the aristocratic free Negroes, they observed, "Some of them were pointed out . . . as very wealthy, but no money can admit them to the pit, or to the boxes."[30]

Whites and Negroes were segregated in the less prestigious public facilities as well. The city jails kept white and black prisoners in separate quarters and dressed them in uniforms of different colors. On August 11, 1836, the city council extended the racial disparity to labor details by adopting an ordinance requiring slaves and free Negroes jailed for longer than three days to be put to work "cleaning and repairing the streets and public roads or levees, or on any other public work."[31] No companion legisla-

Past as Prelude: New Orleans, 1718–1968, ed. Hodding Carter (New Orleans, 1968), p. 217.

28. Thomas Low Nichols, *Forty Years of American Life, 1821–1861* (New York, 1937), pp. 355–56.

29. Sir Charles Lyell, *A Second Visit to the United States of North America* (New York, 1849), II, p. 94.

30. Ferencz A. Pulszky and Theresa Pulszky, *White, Red, Black Sketches of American Society in the United States during the Visit of Their Guests* (New York, 1853), II, p. 101.

31. Calhoun, *Digest of the Ordinances, 1840*, p. 253; Wade, *Slavery in the Cities*, p. 268.

tion was enacted to cover the duties of the white prisoners, who were apparently spared the humiliation of being paraded through the streets of the city in convict clothing.

Segregation of the races on streetcars was not required by city ordinance during the antebellum period, but it was maintained as company policy from the time the cars were placed in service in New Orleans in the 1820s. Some of the omnibus lines excluded blacks altogether, but others operated special cars, easily identified by large black stars painted on to prevent confusion, for Negro passengers.[32] This practice gave rise to local use of the adjective *star* to denote all varieties of separate Negro accommodations, much as the label *Jim Crow* would later become a part of the semantics of segregation on a wider basis.

White restaurants and saloons were strictly segregated by local custom and management policies in New Orleans, as they were throughout the antebellum South.[33] Hotels and inns were also off limits to Negroes, but accommodations were usually provided for black governesses, maids, and other personal attendants traveling with white families. None of the local private clubs and New Orleans chapters of national fraternal organizations admitted Negroes to their ranks. Throughout the antebellum period, the free Negroes who sought club camaraderie and could pay for the privilege founded a large number of lodges and benevolent societies of their own.[34]

Free Negro education developed in a similar way. Excluded from the white private schools since early in the eighteenth century, the children of the New Orleans *gens de couleur* were also denied admission into the new public school system that developed in the city during the 1840s. Compelled to fall back upon their own resources, the free Negroes instituted and supported many private schools of their own, varying from exclusive acad-

32. New Orleans *Daily Picayune*, Nov. 9, 1864.
33. Wade, *Slavery in the Cities*, pp. 266–67.
34. Everett, "Free Persons of Color," p. 258.

emies in the best Continental tradition to such charity schools as the famous École des Orphelins Indigents, generously endowed by Thomy Lafon, Aristide Mary, and other prominent free Negro benefactors.[35]

The Charity Hospital of Louisiana, located in New Orleans, opened its doors to sick whites and Negroes alike, but segregated the races internally. Serving the medical needs of an international seaport, its clientele included patients "of every age and sex, of every color, from the blue-eyed, fair-browed Anglo-American, to the tawn, sun-browned child of the Tropics," according to a visitor to the hospital in 1859.[36] In the antebellum period, before rapidly increasing Negro admissions led to the adoption of entirely separate wings for whites and blacks, segregation was maintained on a ward-by-ward basis. On the eve of the Civil War, Charity Hospital operated three of its eleven surgical wards for the care of Negro patients.[37]

In antebellum New Orleans, the color line extended to the grave. On March 5, 1835, a longstanding local practice was written into law when the city council adopted an ordinance zoning the municipal cemeteries into three parts, allocating one-half of the space for whites, one-fourth for slaves, and one-fourth for free Negroes.[38] Six years later, cemetery segregation was carried a step further by an ordinance requiring separate burial registration lists for whites and Negroes.[39]

The color line was applied conscientiously to most public pursuits throughout the antebellum period in New Orleans. Free

35. Betty Porter, "The History of Negro Education in Louisiana," *Louisiana Historical Quarterly*, XXV (July, 1942), p. 731.

36. Quoted in A. E. Fossier, *The Charity Hospital of Louisiana* (New Orleans, 1923), p. 30.

37. Stella O'Connor, "The Charity Hospital at New Orleans: An Administrative and Financial History, 1736–1941" (M.A. thesis, Tulane University, 1947), p. 94.

38. Wade, *Slavery in the Cities*, pp. 270–71; King, *New Orleans, the Place and the People*, p. 399.

39. *A Digest of the Ordinances and Resolutions of the General Council of the City of New Orleans* (New Orleans, 1845), p. 6.

Negroes and slaves were systematically excluded from white accommodations and social activities and were restricted to separate and usually second-class quarters in the public facilities to which they were admitted. The system fulfilled its immediate purpose rather well, for it removed any danger that unwilling whites would be forced into unwanted physical contact with Negroes in public places, but it had its limitations. While the segregation code prohibited the Negroes from crossing the color line, it was virtually powerless to prevent whites who so desired from mixing at will with the blacks in Negro dance halls, coffee-houses, bawdy houses, and private quarters. In these back-alley activities with which New Orleans was so copiously endowed the segregation system broke down completely.

The countless taverns or grogshops catering illegally but openly to thirsty Negroes often brought whites and blacks together in the brotherhood of John Barleycorn. According to outraged complaints in the New Orleans newspapers, white men and boys frequented such saloons "to revel and dance . . . for whole nights with a lot of men and women of saffron color, or quite black, either slave or free."[40] According to the "city intelligence" column of the *Daily Picayune*, one such "intolerable nuisance" on the corner of Baronne and Perdido streets nightly entertained "a mixed assemblage of slaves, free negroes, and disreputable whites of both sexes."[41] In these grogshops, in private rooms, and in sequestered lofts and garages, whites and Negroes often congregated over dominoes, dice, cards, or a pair of fighting game-cocks.[42]

Men and women in search of clandestine sexual adventures commonly transgressed the color line. The practice of *placage*, the more or less permanent relationships between affluent white men and free black women, was in vogue in New Orleans at the

40. Quoted in Kmen, "Music of New Orleans," p. 214.
41. New Orleans *Daily Picayune*, Apr. 1, 1855.
42. *Ibid.*, June 12, 1852; Feb. 20, June 10, 1855; Reinders, *End of an Era*, p. 165.

time.[43] Far more common, however, were the more casual dalliances between Negroes and whites in the shabbier brothels and back-alley "cribs." Although most of these interracial affairs naturally involved white men and Negro prostitutes, some bawdy houses offered white and black women to all clients regardless of race.[44] One such establishment, located next to the home of United States Senator Pierre Soule on Basin Street, annoyed the venerable lawmaker so much that he filed a complaint against the den of iniquity "where whites and blacks meet indiscriminately" and "make the night the accomplice of their vices and the time for their hellish amusements."[45]

Liaisons between black men and white women beyond the scope of prostitution occasionally came to public attention. Many of them were rather squalid affairs, like that of the white woman and free Negro man apprehended in June, 1855, for "carrying the depravity of Dauphine street even beyond its recognized extent."[46] Others gave every indication of genuine affection. One white woman, arrested in New Orleans in 1852 for living with a fugitive slave, reportedly held in her arms "a mulatto male child, about two years of age," on whom she was lavishing "all the endearments of a mother."[47] Whatever the circumstances, these unions between white women and black men constituted the most flagrant possible defiance of the prerogatives of the master race.

Many white New Orleanians feared that the very foundations of their social order were endangered by such violations of the

43. The intricacies of these alliances are discussed at some length in Everett, "Free Persons of Color," pp. 202–9.

44. New Orleans *Daily Picayune*, June 30, July 1, 18, Aug. 7, 1855; New Orleans *Bee*, July 14, 1853; Reinders, *End of an Era*, p. 166; Herbert Asbury, *The French Quarter: An Informal History of the New Orleans Underworld* (New York, 1938), p. 388.

45. New Orleans *Daily Picayune*, Aug. 7, 1855.

46. *Ibid.*, June 30, July 1, 1855.

47. *Ibid.*, July 24, 1852.

color line. The Negroes, they reasoned, would hardly stand in awe of the white race if they drank and danced and gambled with whites and even on rare occasions enjoyed the favors of a white woman. Moreover, this surreptitious mixing of the races posed a very real threat to the institution of slavery. Not only would such clandestine contacts "corrupt" the slaves, they would also provide perfect opportunities for white troublemakers to spread the insidious doctrines of abolitionism among the servile population.

The first attack upon color-line transgressions was aimed at the quadroon balls, by all accounts the most celebrated of all interracial activities carried on in the city. Free Negro dances had attracted large numbers of eager white men since the colonial period, but the quadroon ball did not develop until 1805, when a dance-hall proprietor named Auguste Tessier began holding two balls a week limited to white men and free black women. The idea proved enormously successful, and the quadroon ball soon established itself as one of New Orleans's most popular activities. White men flocked to the dances for an easy liaison, an introduction that might lead into *placage*, or simply the pleasure of an evening of dancing free from the strictures of white cotillion etiquette.

But the balls soon collected a host of implacable enemies. Strait-laced critics mourned the decline of traditional morality, and color-line guardians somberly prophesied the collapse of southern civilization. Many white women, perhaps infuriated when too many eligible escorts began to forsake "the white privets to gather black grapes,"[48] joined in the mounting chorus against the balls. Apparently a majority of city councilmen accepted the alarmists' warnings or found it impossible to withstand the feminine pique, for they adopted a measure on January 4, 1828, forbidding white

48. Quoted in Kmen, "Music of New Orleans," p. 214.

men, with or without masks, from attending "dressed or masked balls composed of men and women of color."[49] This ordinance, however, did little to dampen male enthusiasm for the balls. Only sporadic efforts were made to enforce it, and the council abandoned its attempts to legislate against mixed amusements for nearly thirty years.

During the 1850s the escalating sectional conflict brought re-newed endeavors to curb contacts between whites and Negroes. As tensions mounted and forebodings of plots against the peculiar institution became a common fixation, white New Orleanians grew increasingly suspicious of all activities that brought the races together beyond the surveillance of the authorities. Their fears were not altogether fanciful. The abrasive, largely autonomous Negro community provided an excellent environment for future Nat Turners or Denmark Veseys. Many whites obviously har-bored no affection for slavery, for *Uncle Tom's Cabin* was hawked openly on the city streets throughout the decade.[50] Even geography conspired to cause worry, for a port city in the very heart of the slave South was an ideal location for an insurrection or an ocean-going underground railroad. In short, there was a very real danger that New Orleans might develop into a mecca for antislavery intrigue.

White fears found expression in a series of new segregation decrees aimed directly at the surreptitious pleasures which most flagrantly ignored or defied the conventions of the color line. A pair of ordinances enacted in December, 1856, and January, 1857, tried to put a stop to the mixed gambling in Negro coffeehouses. The measure adopted on December 13, 1856, prohibited tavern owners or proprietors from letting "white persons and colored persons . . . play cards together, or any other game in their house."[51] If such interracial activities were brought to the atten-

49. Calhoun, *Digest of the Ordinances, 1840*, p. 128; Warfield, *Digest of the Acts, 1848*, p. 145.
50. Chenault and Reinders, "Northern-Born Community," pp. 244–45.
51. Henry J. Leovy, comp., *The Laws and General Ordinances of the*

tion of the authorities, the unfortunate barkeep could be fined as much as one hundred dollars. The companion legislation passed three weeks later set the punishments for the participants. Convicted whites and free Negroes could be fined from twenty-five to one hundred dollars, and guilty slaves were to be assessed fifteen lashes.[52] Two months later the city council turned to the problem of interracial promiscuity. An ordinance adopted on March 10, 1857, outlawed racially integrated bawdy houses. It prohibited white and Negro women "notoriously abandoned to lewdness" from living in the same dwelling and also barred free people of color from lodging white prostitutes.[53]

After Louisiana left the Union and hostilities began, fears of possible fifth-column activities in their midst led white New Orleanians to further intensify surveillance of suspicious contacts between whites and Negroes. The results occasionally assumed ridiculous proportions. In May, 1861, Dr. Thomas Jinnings, a prominent free Negro physician and Sunday-school teacher, took his wife to a charity fair sponsored by the white Episcopal church with which his Sunday school was affiliated. Jinnings was promptly jailed and charged with "intrading [sic] himself among the white congregation . . . and conducting hisself [sic] in a manner unbecoming the free colored population of this city, and in a manner to create insubordination among the servile population of this State."[54] The charges were dropped and Jinnings was released only after some white parishioners testified that the physician had behaved properly and that the couple had been invited to the bazaar by one of the white women in the congregation.

As their actions after the Union occupation would indicate pointedly, many New Orleans Negroes, especially some of the

City of New Orleans, Together with the Acts of the Legislature, Decisions of the Supreme Court, and Constitutional Provisions, Relating to the City Government (New Orleans, 1857), p. 46.
52. *Ibid.*, pp. 260–61.
53. *Ibid.*, p. 378.
54. New Orleans *Daily Picayune*, May 30, 1861.

haughtier *gens de couleur*, bitterly resented the segregation codes and practices that defined their subordinate station in virtually every public place and activity. Their discontent was demonstrated in July, 1833, when a group of Negroes headed for Lake Pontchartrain mounted an armed attack on a white street car that refused to carry them.[55] But manifestations of their frustration were largely limited to such sporadic outbursts, for they lacked the power to do much else.

By the time the guns of war brought the antebellum era to its abrupt end, racial segregation had already reached an advanced stage of development in New Orleans, the only place in Louisiana where the institution of slavery did not guarantee the subordination of the Negroes. In the troubled years ahead, segregation would take on a new importance in the city and country alike as white Louisianians would struggle to maintain their privileged place in a society shaken by the emancipation of the slaves.

55. New Orleans *Argus*, Aug. 1, 1833, quoted in *Niles' Weekly Register*, Aug. 24, 1833.

TWO

The Interregnum, 1862-67

The old order died by degrees in Louisiana. Six chaotic years transpired between the Union conquest of New Orleans in April, 1862, and the final restoration of civilian rule in the state under the Radical Republicans in April, 1868. In rapid succession provisional governments were formed and disbanded, each too short-lived to make Louisiana over in its own image. The drift and confusion of the interregnum years was most apparent in the area of race relations, where the abolition of slavery destroyed irrevocably the old absolutes. The death of the peculiar institution triggered drastic changes in the antebellum legal, economic, and political systems.

The national Republican leaders, after much frenetic infighting, reached agreement on the basic nature of most of these reforms. They determined that the freedmen would be governed by civil law, not personal fiat, and that their labor would be given due financial compensation. In time, when it became obvious to the ruling Radicals that their own interests and Negro liberties would best be safeguarded by Republican control of the southern state governments, the freedmen were also given the vote. But there was no Radical consensus on the more sensitive question of the Negro's social position. Ardent idealists like Thaddeus Stevens and Charles Sumner interpreted the war as a perfect opportunity to eradicate caste distinctions from every facet of southern society. Other Republicans, however, balked at the idea of a racial upheaval, endorsing Abraham Lincoln's belief that "there is a physical difference between the white and black races which . . . will forever forbid the two races living together on terms of social and political equality."[1]

The divided mind of the North on this matter was clearly reflected by the so-called carpetbaggers who came to Louisiana during and after the war. Missionary activities enticed such crusading clergymen as Methodists L. C. Matlack and J. C. Hartzell south to New Orleans to preach the gospel of the brotherhood of man. Union army veterans who remained in the state to take positions with the Freedmen's Bureau included Thomas W. Conway of New York, who later directed school integration efforts as state superintendent of public education, and Ephraim S. Stoddard of Vermont, who tried to carry out Conway's policies as a divisional superintendent in the southwestern parishes. Stoddard expressed the liberal vision eloquently when he proclaimed in a letter to his brother, "The *Typical American*, when he comes as come he will, must be the result of the blending and fusing of every nation and every race created by God. . . . *A unified race*—what a thought! The idea excites the power of my mind to follow. When its completion has been wrought—then is the millenium."

Other northerners in occupied Louisiana were decidedly less euphoric over the idea of racial equality. Many Union officers despised blacks and abused them whenever they had the opportunity. General Benjamin F. Butler, who did little else to win the hearts of local whites, personally quashed a free Negro campaign to desegregate the New Orleans public schools in 1862.[2] His successor, Major General Nathaniel P. Banks, was an avowed

---

1. From Lincoln's fourth debate with Stephen A. Douglas at Charleston, Ill., Sept. 18, 1858, quoted in Philip Van Doren Stern, ed., *The Life and Writings of Abraham Lincoln* (New York, 1940), pp. 492–93.
2. Douglas M. Hall, "Public Education in Louisiana during the War between the States with Special Reference to New Orleans" (M.A. thesis, Louisiana State University, 1940), pp. 67–68.

white supremacist who repeatedly interfered in Unionist political affairs during 1863 and 1864 to prevent the pro-Negro faction from gaining control of the provisional government.[3] Many civilians, including a number of Freedmen's Bureau personnel, became anti-Negro as the apparent hopelessness of their endeavors disillusioned them.

With the northern conquerors so divided on the Negro's proper "place" in the new southern society, much of the impetus in finding a solution was left to the native whites and blacks. Most whites understood that emancipation was the high price they must pay for losing the war, but this realization did little to ameliorate their racist ideology. A Tensas Parish planter spoke for many white Louisianians in 1866 when he told J. T. Trowbridge: "I think God intended the niggers to be slaves; we have the Bible for that. Now since man has deranged God's plan, I think the best we can do is keep 'em as near a state of bondage as possible."[4] The reluctance of many Louisiana Negroes to accept such a lowly station led inevitably to a bitter struggle that continued unabated throughout the reconstruction period.

The race question played a prominent role in Unionist politics beginning in the spring of 1864. Although much of Louisiana was still held by the Confederates, President Lincoln was anxious to begin the process of restoration as quickly as possible. Two elections were scheduled: one in February to elect a governor and other state officials and another in March to choose delegates to a constitutional convention. The loyalists, united under Confederate rule by their opposition to secession, split into three factions after the federal occupation. Conservative Unionists categorically rejected every extension of Negro liberties, includ-

3. Gerald M. Capers, *Occupied City: New Orleans under the Federals, 1862–1865* (Lexington, Ky., 1965), pp. 129–37; John Rose Ficklen, *History of Reconstruction in Louisiana through 1868* (Baltimore, 1910), pp. 45–66.

4. John T. Trowbridge, *A Picture of the Desolated States and the Work of Restoration, 1865–1868* (Hartford, 1868), p. 392.

ing emancipation without compensation to loyal slaveholders. A radical wing favored immediate emancipation and first-class citizenship for Negroes, including the right to vote. The moderate Unionists, led by German-born New Orleans lawyer Michael Hahn, supported emancipation but flatly rejected political and social equality for the blacks.[5]

Race was the only real issue in a thoroughly scurrilous campaign. The conservative ticket never really had a chance, for most of the militant negrophobes were Confederate sympathizers, and many of those who had remained loyal to the Union refused to sign the oath of allegiance required of all registered voters. The election became a two-way encounter between Hahn's moderates and the radicals, led by gubernatorial candidate Benjamin Flanders, an ally of the departed Butler. General Banks, who succeeded "the Beast" as occupational commander, feared that pacification would be endangered by a provisional government in the hands of the radicals, and he used his enormous influence to assure their defeat. Hahn purchased the New Orleans *True Delta* in January and used the newspaper throughout the campaign to feed voters a steady diet of dire prophecies that the preservation of the white race in Louisiana depended upon his election. The strategy evidently impressed the voters, for Hahn and his ticket won a landslide victory in February, and the moderate faction captured most of the constitutional convention seats five weeks later.

The convention, which began its deliberations on April 6, 1864, was in many respects a bastard body. It represented only one faction of the Unionist minority elected only from areas under federal occupation. But on the race question almost all of the delegates reflected the rabid negrophobia of the great majority of white Louisianians. They abolished slavery in the state but petitioned Congress for compensation for loyal slaveholders. They approved a resolution forever prohibiting Negroes

5. Capers, *Occupied City*, pp. 125–41.

from voting in Louisiana but later withdrew it under strong pressure from General Banks and Governor Hahn, who knew that President Lincoln wanted a limited extension of the franchise to Negroes and that the powerful Radical Republican faction in Congress might oppose the new constitution if it sanctioned a lily-white electorate. Despite the pressure, however, all that the delegates were willing to concede was a loophole permitting the legislature to enfranchise Negroes in the future if it so desired.[6]

On June 30, the heretofore latent issue of integration exploded during a debate over a proposal to extend public education to all children, regardless of race. Delegate Edmund Abell of New Orleans, spokesman for the small conservative contingent and a rabid white supremacist, took the floor to "fight every proposition that looks to the commingling of the colored with the white race." Lecturing the convention that "contact with a race which God has marked differently from the white race is sure to cause the downfall of one or the other," Abell argued that the ambiguity of the resolution might later lead to the admission of black children into the same schools as white children. His objection was supported, and the proposal was overwhelmingly rejected despite an eloquent plea by Alfred C. Hills, a New Orleans moderate, that the real issue was training Negroes to become enlightened and productive citizens, not the mixing of the races.[7]

Many of the delegates were not only opposed to mixed schools but they also disapproved of "negro children being educated, at the present time, by taxation on white property holders," as John Sullivan of New Orleans expressed it. J. R. Terry, also of New Orleans, proposed a plan segregating the school systems by sources of revenue, with white schools financed by white property taxes and black schools supported by a head tax on Negroes. A thinly veiled attempt to hopelessly cripple black edu-

6. Ficklen, *History of Reconstruction in Louisiana*, pp. 70–72.
7. *Debates in the Convention for the Revision and Amendment of the Constitution of the State of Louisiana* (New Orleans, 1864), pp. 493, 495, 499.

cation, it was approved by a voice vote. It stood until July 18, when Judge Abell read the delegates a letter from A. P. Dostie, a prominent New Orleans Radical Republican, protesting the writing of such terms as "white," "black," and "color" into the constitution. He recommended that the convention simply enact a measure providing public education to all children from six to eighteen, not mentioning race at all. The delegates once again demonstrated vulnerability to outside pressure. On July 22, only three weeks after they had convincingly rejected a similar proposal, they adopted the Dostie recommendation fifty to twenty-nine, with Abell and Sullivan leading the last-ditch opposition.[8]

The constitution of 1864 thus abolished slavery, left-handedly sanctioned black public education, and passed the problem of Negro suffrage on to future lawmakers. But the Unionists had no real opportunity to put their racial ideas into practice, for the collapse of the Confederacy in 1865 necessitated new elections on a more truly statewide basis. After eighteen months in office, they were swept out by the Democratic landslide of November 6, 1865. Unlike the Unionists, the Louisiana Democrats were not divided or ambiguous on the race question. They considered blacks inferior to whites in every way and believed that the Negro's natural station in society was at the very mudsill. The Democratic platform of 1865 expressed this creed unmistakably when it demanded a "Government of white people, made and to be perpetuated for the exclusive benefit of the white race" and declared that "there can, in no event, nor under any circumstances, be any equality between the white and other races."[9]

The new Democratic legislature missed an opportunity to write its ideology into state law when it convened on November 25, 1865, to enact the so-called Louisiana black code. Bills proposing the auctioning of unemployed freedmen to private bidders and

8. *Ibid.*, pp. 501, 502, 575, 601.
9. Quoted in Walter L. Fleming, ed., *Documentary History of Reconstruction* (Cleveland, 1906), I, p. 229.

requiring agricultural workers to sign annual contracts were abandoned after they aroused the wrath of Radicals in Congress. The only important bill passed during the special session, a vagrancy law, made no mention of race. A bill was introduced giving the freedmen the same legal status as that of the free Negroes before the war, but it was abandoned in the rush to adjourn. During the regular session of 1866, a senate committee reported that such a measure was not necessary "in view of the humane provisions of the law of Louisiana which existed long anterior to the late war, and which extends to all free persons alike the right to hold property, testify in courts , acquire education, etc."[10]

If the Democrats were unwilling to write their racial philosophy into state law, where it would certainly attract the attention of the hostile Radicals in Congress, they revealed no such reluctance in their public school policies. Robert Mills Lusher, a native of South Carolina who had served before the war as a New Orleans school director and during the conflict as a member of the Confederate "Louisiana Guards," was elected state superintendent of public education. An unyielding white supremacist, Lusher refused to consider schools for Negroes as a part of his duties. In a letter to parish school officials, he leveled a savage attack on Governor J. Madison Wells for reviving the old idea of spending Negro tax revenues on schools for black children. This, according to Lusher, amounted to "counseling an absolute neglect of all indigent white children ... while suggesting that provision be made for the mental training of an inferior race." His goal as superintendent, he explained in a circular letter to parish assessors, was to assure "the future honor and prosperity of Louisiana ... and the supremacy of the Caucasian race in her councils." To the sheriffs, Lusher pledged to work for schools that would "vindicate the honor and supremacy of the Caucasian race."[11]

10. Quoted in Ficklen, *History of Reconstruction in Louisiana*, p. 144.
11. *Report of the Superintendent of Public Education, to the General*

Denied access to state facilities, Negroes depended almost entirely upon the schools maintained by the federal government and missionary societies. The first attempt to build a school system for black children came in January, 1863, when General Banks sponsored formation of a freedmen's education committee. By December, 1864, nearly ten thousand Negroes attended ninety-five schools supported and operated by the military in parishes under federal control. With the creation of the Bureau of Refugees, Freedmen, and Abandoned Lands by Congress in 1865, that agency gradually supplanted the army's educational efforts in Louisiana. Although plagued continually by financial difficulties and personnel problems, the Freedmen's Bureau schools operated as the Negro version of the Lusher system until the state assumed control of black education in 1867 and 1868.[12]

Excluded from the polls and the public schools, Louisiana Negroes were also strictly segregated in their use of public transportation and recreational facilities. Steamboats continued to separate their passengers by color, as did the New Orleans streetcars. Negroes were excluded from public halls, theatres, and concerts or were required to sit in balconies. White ballrooms, coffee-houses, and restaurants would not accept black patronage. Some New Orleans merchants even refused to sell dry goods to Negroes across the counter.[13] These practices provoked one caustic black editor to speculate: "Suppose we have a colored man as Mayor. He will be ejected from theatres, fairs, concerts, and most of the places of public resort. . . . Suppose we have colored police officers . . . and a crime is committed in a coffee-house whose owner wants to admit white people only."[14]

Thus the proper station in society for the Negro, according to Louisiana's Unionists and Democrats alike, was a lowly one,

---

Assembly of the State of Louisiana, 1865 (New Orleans, 1866), pp. 16, 17, 23, cited hereafter as *Report of the Superintendent*, by year.
  12. Porter, "Negro Education in Louisiana," pp. 738, 740–46.
  13. New Orleans *Tribune*, Apr. 4, May 16, June 19, 30, 1867.
  14. *Ibid.*, June 19, 1867.

ostracized from the polls and public schools and segregated into shabby, second-class public accommodations. The first Negroes to protest against this subordination were such proud, articulate New Orleans *gens de couleur* as Aristide Mary, Thomy Lafon, Paul Trevigne, and the Roudanez brothers, J. B. and Louis. Soon after the Union conquest of New Orleans they had begun a determined bid to win the right to vote and access for their children to white public schools. Assisted by Trevigne's short-lived newspaper *L'Union* and later by the New Orleans *Tribune*, owned and edited by the Roudanez brothers, they argued cogently that their property holdings, learning, and loyalty to the Union entitled them to first-class citizenship. At first they had been tempted to disassociate themselves from the humbler free Negroes and the lowly freedmen, but they soon realized that emancipation had made internal distinctions obsolete. As one of them told Whitelaw Reid in the summer of 1865: "We see that our future is indissolubly bound up with that of the negro race in this country; and we have resolved to make common cause and rise or fall with them. We have no rights which we can reckon safe while the same are denied field-hands on the sugar plantations."[15] Once united with other Louisiana Negroes, this "colored Creole" elite assumed a disproportionate share of the leadership in the civil rights crusades during the reconstruction period.

Like their quest for the franchise, the Negro struggle against segregation began several years before the Radical Republicans came to power in Louisiana. Predictably, this agitation began in New Orleans, where talented leadership, highly developed public accommodations, and a certain white indifference combined to create a highly promising environment for protest. In the country parishes, where no powerful black leadership developed and public accommodations were nonexistent or unimportant, segregation did not become a source of controversy between the

15. Whitelaw Reid, *After the War: A Tour of the Southern States, 1865–1866* (Cincinnati, 1866), p. 244.

races until the constitution of 1868 made it one. In New Orleans, however, the color line in the public schools and other municipal facilities came under attack shortly after the Union conquest of the city.

In September, 1862, a light-skinned free Negro girl was mistakenly permitted to enroll in the Barracks School. When her ancestry was discovered, principal Josephine Mettasca expelled her, and the Fourth District School Board hurriedly adopted a resolution forbidding the admission of Negroes to their schools. The girl's mother brought the matter to the attention of General Butler, who ordered the girl reinstated immediately. When board officials refused to alter their policy, Butler summoned them for a hearing. They agreed to appoint a committee to investigate the situation, but it accomplished nothing and its members resigned rather than recommend school integration. Butler, occupied with problems of his own and understandably reluctant to add to his troubles with the white community, allowed the matter to be dropped.[16] School segregation policies remained a target for black critics, especially the New Orleans *Tribune*, but no actual protest movement developed during the interregnum.

Segregated streetcars provided the Negroes with their first real opportunity to wage war against the color line in New Orleans. The star car system had infuriated many Negroes since its inception and had provoked the only violent confrontation over segregation during the whole antebellum period. Shortly after the Union occupation began, a delegation of prominent free Negroes called upon General Butler and asked him to desegregate the streetcars. Butler ordered the omnibus lines to accept black passengers on all cars, but the decree was challenged by the car companies and set aside by a local court. When Butler was replaced by the less sympathetic Banks in December, 1862, the

16. Hall, "Public Education in Louisiana," pp. 67–68; Leon O. Beasley, "A History of Education in Louisiana During the Reconstruction Period, 1862–1877" (Ph.D. dissertation, Louisiana State University, 1957), pp. 37–38.

free Negroes temporarily abandoned the streetcar issue to concentrate on winning the vote.[17]

The controversy was revived during the summer of 1864 after Banks received complaints from some of his black troops that they were being discriminated against by the car lines. He met with company officials and persuaded them to let black soldiers ride on all cars, but the Negro civilians remained restricted to the star cars. This dichotomy enraged local black leaders. In January, 1865, Charles E. Logan and Dr. R. W. Rogers urged formation of a committee to draft a petition to military authorities protesting "the restrictions imposed upon the colored people, preventing them from riding in the city cars." Another black critic thought it "a shame that a colored soldier be received in the cars, and his mother be expelled." Even black military personnel joined in the outcry. Demanding that "no distinction be made between citizens and soldiers," Captain W. B. Barrett urged Negroes, "We must claim the right of riding for every one of us, and claim it unconditionally."[18]

Their pleas met with temporary success in August, 1865, when they persuaded Major E. R. S. Canby, commander of the Department of the Gulf, to issue a directive stating that "the attempt to enforce police laws or regulations that discriminate against negroes by reason of color, or their former condition of slavery... will not be permitted."[19] The New Orleans *Tribune* elatedly informed its readers that "the distinction between 'star cars' and 'no star' is no longer of any value" and reported that black passengers were being accepted "with little or no difficulty" on all of the city lines.[20] The celebration proved premature, however, for once again the car companies took the matter to the courts. Only two weeks after the Canby directive had been put into effect it was invalidated by United States Provost

17. New Orleans *Tribune*, Jan. 13, 1865.
18. *Ibid.*
19. *Ibid.*, Aug. 20, 1865.
20. *Ibid.*

Judge Benedict, who ruled that the order infringed upon the basic right of a private corporation to refuse service to any group or individual it so desired.[21] Once again approximately one-third of the streetcars were decorated with large black stars, and segregation was restored as official company policy.

In addition to the obvious humiliation it engendered, the star system worked to the disadvantage of Negroes in a practical sense. While they were excluded from most of the vehicles, their own star cars were often usurped by impatient whites. Commenting on this practice in November, 1864, the New Orleans *Daily Picayune* noted sarcastically, "White persons can ride in the 'star' cars if they choose, but they have no right to object to the presence of darkeys there." In September, 1865, "A Citizen" complained to the New Orleans *Times* that on Sundays the cars running on Canal Street—both white and star—were usually taken over completely by whites, excluding the Negroes altogether. The condition was not alleviated, for the New Orleans *Crescent*, certainly no advocate of racial equality, observed in May, 1867, that "it constantly occurs that white men, women and children fill the star cars, to the exclusion of colored persons, and it is a spectacle frequently seen, that white persons occupy the seats in these cars, while colored persons of both sexes are compelled to ride standing in the aisles."[22]

The controversy finally erupted in the spring of 1867. In April the *Tribune* intensified its attacks against the star system. Chiding the segregationists for their reluctance to face up to the inevitability of social change, the *Tribune* declared: "All these discriminations that had slavery at the bottom have become nonsense. It behooves those who feel bold enough to shake off the old prejudice and to confront their prejudiced associates, to show their hands."[23] Radical Republican orators, hoping to convert

21. New Orleans *Times*, Sept. 3, 1865.
22. New Orleans *Daily Picayune*, Nov. 9, 1864; New Orleans *Times*, Sept. 3, 1865; New Orleans *Daily Crescent*, May 7, 1867.
23. New Orleans *Tribune*, Apr. 21, 1867.

black discontent into a massive bloc vote, found streetcar segregation a very timely issue.

On Sunday, April 28, words gave way to action. William Nichols, a Negro, boarded a white car and was forcibly removed by car starter Edward Cox. Nichols was arrested for a breach of the peace, but two days later the city recorder, evidently anxious to avert widespread trouble, dismissed the charges on the grounds of insufficient evidence. Nichols, who apparently incited the fracas to precipitate a confrontation over streetcar policies, was unwilling to let the affair die. He promptly countersued Cox for assault and battery.[24]

The Cox-Nichols incident triggered a chain reaction of Negro attempts to challenge the color line on the white cars. This presented the car companies with a delicate problem, for they wanted to retain segregation without running the risk of violence or lawsuits. They tried to resolve the dilemma with a policy of "passive resistance." Streetcar personnel were instructed not to assault black intruders, however great the provocation, but they were ordered not to start the car on its way until the Negroes tired of the game and left the car. This strategy was put to a practical test on Friday, May 3, when a black man named P. Ducloslange boarded a white car on St. Charles Avenue. Ducloslange was not ejected, but the car remained stationary. Some of the white passengers departed when the Negro boarded, others left during the delay, and it soon developed into a sitzkrieg between Ducloslange and the driver. After more than an hour, the Negro departed and the car proceeded on its route, victorious but empty.[25]

The weekend of May 4–5 brought New Orleans to the brink of race warfare. On Saturday a bellicose crowd of black men and boys gathered on Love Street, in the Third Municipal Dis-

24. New Orleans *Times*, May 1, 1867; New Orleans *Daily Crescent*, May 9, 1867. After settlement of the car controversy, Nichols dropped charges against Cox, explaining that his sole objective had been to bring company policies to a legal test.
25. New Orleans *Tribune*, May 1, 4, 1867.

trict, and began harassing the passing white cars by shouting
curses, blocking the street, and showering the cars with bottles,
bricks, and other available projectiles. A leader of the mob, Joseph
Guillaume, jumped aboard a white car and defiantly refused to
leave. When the enraged driver forgot his instructions and tried
to eject the Negro bodily, Guillaume overpowered him, seized
the reins, and began to make off with the street car as a trophy
of war while the terrified passengers evacuated as best they could.
Guillaume was finally captured by Third District police after
a spirited chase and was taken into custody.[26]

The crowd grew angrier, and the arrival of the police only
seemed to make matters worse. Sergeant Strong of the Third District station reported to Chief of Police Thomas E. Adams that
"squads of colored men, fifteen or twenty in a gang, armed with
clubs, are gathering on Love Street, jumping on the cars and
making threats toward the drivers." A short time later Officer
Kiernan, desk clerk at the Treme station, described the fracas
to Adams as "a large crowd of colored men in open riot."[27] Police
units from neighboring stations reinforced the beleaguered Third
District lawmen, contained the mob, and prevented the violence
from spreading, but tensions remained intense. A *Crescent* reporter thought the "public mind" to be "in a very feverish condition during the day, apprehensions having possessed people
that a serious, perhaps calamitous disturbance might come upon the city, as a result of the continued agitation of this car
question."[28]

On Sunday, May 5, the unrest reached its climax. Early in the
morning D. M. Reid, superintendent of P. G. T. Beauregard's
New Orleans and Carrollton Railroad Company, told Mayor
Edward Heath that his way-station personnel had reported
"threats . . . made by colored persons that they intended to force

26. New Orleans *Times*, May 5, 1867.
27. Quoted in *ibid*.
28. New Orleans *Daily Crescent*, May 7, 1867.

themselves on the cars reserved for white persons . . . and that should the driver resist or refuse them passage, they would compel him to leave the car and take forcible possession themselves." Convinced by events the day before that these threats pointed to "much danger of riotous conduct," Reid urged the mayor to take every possible step to "insure the preservation of the public peace."[29]

Despite the strong possibility of violence, Reid and other omnibus officials decided to keep their cars running and to maintain their strategy of passive resistance. The policy was again tested early in the morning when two black women boarded a white streetcar and adamantly refused to leave, causing the white passengers to disembark. The driver, faithfully executing company procedure, refused to continue on his route, and the increasingly familiar battle of patiences began. But this confrontation went to the Negroes. After a considerable delay, the driver succumbed to his impatience and drove the two triumphant women to their destination.[30] A few more Negroes tried to ride in the cars with less success, but by and large the morning passed with surprising tranquility.

That afternoon the smouldering resentments of generations of subordinate status flamed into open violence. A band of black men tried to force their way onto a white car on Canal Street, but they were driven off by the white passengers after some heated exchanges of insults and fisticuffs. Another group of Negroes jumped aboard a white car on Rampart Street, overpowered the white riders, and forced the terrified driver to parade them past cheering throngs of their fellow protesters. A lone Negro vaulted onto another white omnibus, encouraged by choruses of "stay on, stay on" from the black onlookers lining the sidewalks. Another gang of Negroes tried to take possession of a

29. D. M. Reid to Edward Heath, May 5, 1867, G. T. Beauregard Papers, Louisiana State University Archives.
30. New Orleans *Daily Picayune*, May 7, 1867.

white car, but was repelled by a single white Union soldier, who reportedly informed the blacks at gunpoint that he had a mother and sister and would not tolerate this insult to the white ladies on the car. Throughout the city, scattered fights broke out between roving bands of whites and Negroes.[31]

As the news of the disturbances spread, inevitable transformations took place in the throngs of people, white and Negro, who ventured forth onto the streets. The less bellicose white New Orleanians stayed away from the likely trouble spots, particularly the streetcars. Angry mobs of white men and boys roamed about in search of blacks on whom to vent their wrath. A number of them armed themselves and boarded cars, riding in wait for a Negro attack. The black mobs grew correspondingly larger and bolder, their mood uglier. Their sorties against the white cars were now carried out by small armies wielding such weapons as clubs, bottles, knives, and pistols.

The most massive of the black crowds formed on Rampart Street near Congo Square, the traditional assembly ground for Sunday slave dances during the antebellum period. On this occasion, however, they came for mayhem, not merriment. Earlier in the afternoon some twenty Negroes had "liberated" a white streetcar after a pitched battle and had forced the driver to chauffeur them back and forth in front of a cheering crowd. The excitement brought other blacks to the scene, and still more were called from passing star cars to join their burgeoning ranks. Soon an estimated five hundred Negroes were milling angrily in Congo Square and laying siege to every white streetcar that passed. A number of the blacks boarded the cars, rode triumphantly for a few blocks, then returned to rejoin the Congo Square festivities. Impromptu orators rose up wherever they could attract an audience, haranguing those within earshot with a gospel

31. *Ibid.*; New Orleans *Daily Crescent*, May 7, 1867; New Orleans *Times*, May 7, 1867.

of hate and violence that the mob was only too willing to listen to and act upon.[32]

At this point Mayor Edward Heath decided that the time had come to intervene. Awakened that morning by D. M. Reid's dire warning, Heath had kept a careful watch over the disturbances that now threatened to get out of control. Now a decision had to be made. He might have done nothing, hoping that the riot would burn itself out. But black rage seemed to be mounting, not diminishing, and he feared that the less reputable white elements might soon step in and precipitate a massacre if the officials did not control the Congo Square situation. He might have called in more city police, but he knew that they lacked the manpower to crush the disturbance and feared that their presence would only further enrage the Negroes.[33] His ultimate resort was the occupational forces garrisoned in the city under his good friend General Philip Sheridan, commander of the Fifth Military District. Sheridan's soldiers certainly had the power to quell the riot, but Heath, a moderate Republican, evidently feared the political repercussions from the Congressional Radicals if he were to have the troops deployed against the Negroes.[34] Rejecting a show of force at that time, the mayor courageously decided to go to Congo Square and reason with the crowd personally. If words failed, then and only then would troops be summoned.

Since his appointment to the mayoralty by Sheridan a few months earlier, Heath had won a well-earned reputation among Negroes for fairness. It now served him well. He pleaded with the mob to disperse and return to their homes before a tragedy simi-

32. *Ibid.*
33. Relations between city police and the black community were less than cordial, particularly after the fighting on Love Street the day before.
34. Congressional Radicals had reacted very strongly against the brutal tactics used by city police against the Negroes in the tragic massacre of July 30, 1866, and it would have been easy for Heath's Radical critics to draw a parallel. See Donald E. Reynolds, "The New Orleans Riot of 1866, Reconsidered," *Louisiana History*, V (Winter, 1964), pp. 5–27.

lar to the bloodbath of July 30, 1866, was touched off.[35] He promised the Negroes that the proper authorities would reexamine streetcar policies immediately and that their case would be given serious consideration. His speech was interrupted at several points by jeers and catcalls from some of the diehards, but the apparent sincerity of his pledges defused the martial spirit of the crowd. Soon the square was empty.[36]

On the following day Mayor Heath, General Sheridan, and streetcar executives met to settle the matter. The company spokesmen, hoping to preserve both property and segregation, asked Sheridan to support the star system by posting armed soldiers on every car. Realizing that such a step would only prolong the problem and would embroil the army in a nasty local dispute, the hero of Cedar Creek flatly refused their request. The streetcar officials then withdrew and met alone to forge out a common racial policy. They realized that they might lose a considerable volume of white business if they desegregated the cars, but they knew that they ran the greater risk of losing their property and even more traffic if the disorders were to continue. Finally they took the line of least resistance and agreed to abandon the star system altogether. That evening, drivers and starters were instructed to permit travelers of all colors to ride the cars.[37] To prevent more violence on the cars, Chief of Police Adams warned pointedly, "No passenger has the right to eject any other passenger, no matter what his color. If he does so, he is liable to arrest for assault, or breach of the peace."[38]

The actual death of streetcar segregation came more slowly. On May 8 the *Daily Crescent* reported "very little change" in

35. Thirty-four Negroes had been killed and 119 wounded when the Radicals tried to reconvene the constitutional convention of 1864. See *ibid.*, p. 13.

36. New Orleans *Daily Picayune*, May 7, 1867.

37. *Ibid.*, May 7, 8, 1867; New Orleans *Tribune*, May 7, 1867; New Orleans *Daily Crescent*, May 7, 8, 1867.

38. Thomas E. Adams to Lieutenant Ramel, May 6, 1867, as quoted in the New Orleans *Daily Crescent*, May 7, 1867.

black riding habits. According to the *Crescent*, "Nearly all of the colored travelers still go in the star cars, and even wait for them though a car for whites may be passing or present." Two days later the same newspaper informed its readers that the black passengers "of their own volition, still take the star cars. The cases of negroes entering the cars hitherto assigned to whites are exceptional."[39] But gradually the exceptions became the rule, as the meeker blacks followed their more adventurous kinsmen onto the mixed cars as soon as they realized that havoc would not ensue. After a few weeks the black stars were painted over, obliterating the last visible signs of the old system.

White New Orleanians accepted streetcar desegregation remarkably well. On May 10 a company spokesman happily informed a *Crescent* reporter that the omnibus lines were experiencing "little difference in the amount of travel on the city railroads since the distinction between cars has been abolished."[40] On the night of May 20, a gang of white men armed with pistols and clubs forced their way aboard some mixed cars in the vicinity of the levee and ousted the Negro passengers, injuring one rather seriously.[41] Then the turmoil abated.

Opinions on the importance of the streetcar controversy varied considerably. The *Daily Crescent*, ignoring the underlying causes of the unrest, reported with relief that the matter has been settled and "the probability of a collision of races averted." The *Times*, noting that the star cars had been physically identical to the white ones, condescendingly dismissed the whole conflict as "a clamor for shadows." Even the *Tribune*, the Negro newspaper responsible for much of the agitation against the star system, dismissed the system's downfall as "minor" and began to campaign for the desegregation of the public schools. But the blatantly white supremacist *Daily Picayune* saw more clearly than

39. New Orleans *Daily Crescent*, May 8, 10, 1867.
40. *Ibid.*, May 10, 1867.
41. New Orleans *Tribune*, May 22, 1867.

its competitors that the car controversy was "simply the introductory step to more radical innovations, which must materially alter our whole social fabric." Ominously hinting of a "covert design in the whole movement," the *Picayune* predicted that the "sudden change . . . promises to assume a serious aspect as far as social tranquility and good order is concerned."[42]

It did not take long for the truth in that prophecy to become apparent. A few days after the streetcar companies capitulated, Negroes began to demand service in white coffeehouses, theatres, and retail stores. Coming on the heels of the car disturbances, these new assaults on the color line threatened to further inflame racial tensions. Hoping to avert another crisis, Mayor Heath asked City Attorney Henry D. Ogden for an official opinion. Ogden ruled in favor of the white business interests, basing his argument on a somewhat elastic definition of private property. "Although expecting remuneration from the patronage of the community at large," he wrote, "they are nevertheless private property, owned by private individuals or private corporations, and subject to such rules and regulations as the proprietors may deem proper to adopt." On May 15 Mayor Heath issued a proclamation prohibiting "all persons whatever from intruding into any store, shop or other place of business conducted by private individuals, against the consent and wishes of the owners, proprietors, or keepers of the same."[43] The *Tribune* condemned the action, but no mass protest developed.

By the summer of 1867 it was becoming increasingly apparent that segregation was on the defensive against those "radical innovations." New Orleans Negroes had questioned it in the public schools, challenged it in retail establishments, and destroyed it on the streetcars. The interregnum had not been a period of sweeping social change, but it had been a time of testing. Whites now

42. New Orleans *Daily Crescent*, May 7, 1867; New Orleans *Times*, May 7, 1867; New Orleans *Tribune*, May 9, 1867; New Orleans *Daily Picayune*, May 7, 1867.
43. New Orleans *Tribune*, May 16, June 30, 1867.

knew that the prouder Negroes would not be satisfied with "forty acres and a mule." Negroes had learned the intoxicating lesson that they could bring about social reforms by mass resistance. Both races knew that the conflict over segregation was rapidly developing into a struggle of major proportions as the interregnum gave way to the era of Radical reconstruction in Louisiana.

THREE

The Triumph of the Radicals
1867-68

While Negroes labored in New Orleans to redefine local racial mores, Radical Republicans in Washington were at work destroying the white monopoly on political power throughout the South. As a result of the bitter elections of 1866, the Radicals in both houses of the Congress won majorities large enough to overcome presidential vetoes and enact their own "thorough" reconstruction policies. On March 2, 1867, they voted into law the First Reconstruction Act, reorganizing ten southern states into five military districts under appointed federal commanders, ordering new constitutional conventions, disfranchising Confederate partisans, and decreeing that Negroes be granted the vote. Three weeks later, to negate the possibility that white southerners might prefer military rule indefinitely, Congress enacted a supplemental measure directing the federal commanders to take the initiative in registering voters, electing delegates, and calling conventions. In Louisiana, General Sheridan set in motion voter registration procedures that enrolled 82,907 Negroes and 44,732 whites and called for delegate elections on September 27 and 28, 1867.

These activities provoked some frenzied political maneuvering that rekindled tensions over racial integration. Republican leaders working to secure the support of the newly enfranchised Negroes discovered that public school desegregation evoked considerable black enthusiasm, especially in New Orleans, and they made it into a basic feature of their campaign. The Republican platform of 1867 declared, "We as a party insist on perfect equality, without distinction of race or color," and it promised to "enforce the opening of all schools, from the highest to the lowest . . . to all children."[1] Radical orators reiterated the point at every opportunity. In April a white speaker in New Orleans asked his black audience, "If my colored brother and I touch elbows at the polls, why should not his child and mine stand side by side in the school room?"[2] Two months later Thomas W. Conway assured a Union League rally that the Republicans would provide free schools "to which all children shall be admitted and instructed, regardless of color."[3] These pronouncements elicited the hearty endorsement of the *Tribune*, which chided timorous blacks and hesitant white Republicans by asking: "When will the right time come? Is it, per chance, after we will have separated for ten or twenty years the two races in different schools, and when we shall have realized the separation of this nation into two peoples? . . . It will, then, be TOO LATE."[4]

These desegregationist sentiments terrified white conservatives. Even before the upheavals of 1867, Louisiana whites had been frightened by the slightest possibility of integrated public schools. During the constitutional convention of 1864, an innocuous proposal for separate Negro schools had unleashed a torrent of irrational warnings of impending racial amalgamation. In 1866 the Alexandria *Lousiana Democrat* prophesied that "negro and white children are to be drawn by a leveling process, into a grand Democratic equality in the Republic of letters, through the medium of the Public schools."[5] A few months later a white conservative wrote that the sight of black and white amity at Radical functions

1. Quoted in the New Orleans *Tribune*, June 18, 1867.
2. Quoted in *ibid.*, Apr. 17, 1867.
3. Quoted in *ibid.*, June 5, 1867.
4. *Ibid.*, July 31, 1867.
5. Alexandria *Louisiana Democrat*, Feb. 21, 1866.

"was enough to freeze the blood."[6] By the summer of 1867, after the Radicals had captured control of the federal government and Negroes had desegregated the New Orleans streetcars, white fears mounted. In a letter to St. John R. Liddell, G. H. Williams predicted "the destruction of our institutions and character as a section" and added, "for this the Radicals are now striving unceasingly."[7]

As it became increasingly apparent that the new registration drive would produce a black majority which would no doubt elect a regime committed to school integration, some public school officials decided in desperation to establish their own Negro school systems as a last-ditch defense of the racial homogeneity of their white institutions. In May the New Orleans school board appointed a committee to study the feasibility of creating a parallel system for blacks by taking over the Freedmen's Bureau schools and missionary institutions in the city. In July the board allocated $60,000 for that purpose.[8] During the summer, school boards in the outlying communities of Orleans and Jefferson Parishes made similar plans. The *Tribune* may have been characteristically intemperate, but probably accurate, when it condemned local school officials for "simply looking to keep off colored children from white schools" after having "left them as pariahs on the public streets, while they shamelessly applied the taxes paid by colored parents to educating white children."[9]

Despite such protests, the "star" school systems were instituted in the autumn of 1867. On September 1, the city of Jefferson took over two Freedmen's Bureau schools and began a third, thus creating the first locally operated public school system for Negroes in Louisiana. On October 3, the New Orleans city coun-

6. F. D. Richardson to St. John R. Liddell, July 31, 1866, Moses Liddell and St. John R. Liddell Papers, Louisiana State University Archives.

7. Williams to Liddell, May 21, 1867, Moses Liddell and St. John R. Liddell Papers.

8. New Orleans *Tribune*, May 25, July 24, 1867.

9. *Ibid.*, July 24, 1867.

cil passed an ordinance empowering the school board to set up a Negro school system and allocated a supplemental appropriation of $70,000 to finance the project. In late October, Jefferson Parish followed suit. A week after the New Orleans black school system was authorized, the first two black public schools in the city were opened. By the end of October four more schools were in operation. A few days later the local Freedmen's Bureau officials, overjoyed at the opportunity to diminish their financial burden, turned their sixteen schools over to the city, giving the Negro system twenty-two schools after only five weeks of existence.[10]

Creation of the city-operated black schools infuriated those Negroes who wanted black children absorbed into the white school system. Urging Negroes to settle for nothing less than "a rising generation ... raised as one people," the *Tribune* argued that "a nation cannot have unity and strength, unless all children be educated in the same schools."[11] According to an opinion survey conducted by the *Crescent* in September, many black teachers agreed. E. Tinchaud, principal of a bureau school at 280 St. Claude, was adamantly opposed to segregation and refused to incorporate his school into the city system unless "there be no distinction on account of race or color." Miss E. G. Highgate, a New York Negro teaching in the Free School of the Louisiana Relief Association, thought that desegregation might cause temporary problems "but would ultimate well."[12]

The majority of black teachers interviewed, however, expressed fears over desegregation, prompted perhaps by the unsettling fact that their remarks would be read by a predominantly white audience. P. M. Williams, principal of the bureau school at 300 Gravier, stated that Negro children were entitled to enter

10. Porter, "Negro Education in Louisiana," pp. 745, 750–51; New Orleans *Daily Picayune*, Oct. 12, Nov. 7, 1867; New Orleans *Daily Crescent*, Sept. 15, 17, 1867; Report of the *Superintendent*, 1867–1868, pp. 10–11.
11. New Orleans *Tribune*, July 9, 24, 1867.
12. New Orleans *Daily Crescent*, Sept. 15, 1867.

white schools but warned that "under the circumstances existing in the city at present, it is advisable and for the best interest of all classes that separate schools be established for white and colored children." Another Negro principal pointed out that black students fought continually with the lighter-skinned children of mixed ancestry in her school and predicted that disciplinary problems would be insurmountable if black and white children were placed together. Nelson Pavageaud, a black Freedmen's Bureau official, told the *Crescent* reporter that desegregation might work in the distant future, but now "it would be the very worst thing that could be done."[13]

White teachers in the Negro schools shared these apprehensions. Francis Cote, principal of the Franklin Institute at 258 Rampart Street, told reporters that he had tried to teach a mixed school but was forced to abandon the practice when discipline proved impossible. He categorically stated that "he would not teach both colors in the same school."[14] Miss Cornelia Clarkson, a native New Orleanian in charge of the Lincoln School at 369 Common Street, thought it "inadvisable to mix colored and white children in the same schools," as did northern-born John H. Collins, principal of the bureau school at 318 Gravier. According to Collins, parents of his black pupils had petitioned him to keep his school open if the public schools were mixed. Miss Clarkson told reporters that parents of her pupils had informed her that the desire to desegregate was held only by "those actively engaged in politics or by those so near white that they are unwilling to associate exclusively with colored persons and thereby acknowledge their race."[15]

13. *Ibid.*, Sept. 15, 17, 1867.
14. *Ibid.*, Sept. 15, 1867. This may have been the only school in New Orleans desegregated before the Radicals came to power. Consisting of about fifty children, half black and half white ("mostly children of Frenchmen, a few Italians"), it was plagued by interracial strife until Cote limited admission to Negroes only.
15. *Ibid.*, Sept. 15, 17, 1867.

While the teachers debated the efficacy of school integration in the newspapers, the future course of Louisiana race relations was being determined at the polls. General Sheridan had called for statewide elections on September 27 and 28 to authorize a new constitutional convention and select its delegates. Because federal law at that time stipulated that the convention had to win the approval of a majority of all registered voters, the hopelessly outnumbered whites boycotted the balloting in an effort to perpetuate the lesser evil of military rule indefinitely.[16] But nearly 62 percent of the voters came to the polls and endorsed the convention by the overwhelming margin of 75,083 to 4,006. Of the ninety-eight delegates chosen, all but two were Republicans. There were forty-nine whites and forty-nine Negroes, a ratio previously agreed upon by the Radical leaders to avert the possibility of drafting a constitution unacceptable to the party faithful of either race.[17]

Despite this precaution, the issue of desegregation was simply too explosive to prevent disunity among the Louisiana Republicans, a jerry-built coalition of native white Unionists, northern-born carpetbaggers, and Negroes. A month before the convention opened, some of the white Radicals began to entertain doubts over the practicality of the party's pledge to "enforce the opening of all schools . . . to all children." In October the New Orleans *Republican*, a daily newspaper just founded by Henry Clay Warmoth and other prominent white Radicals, came out in support of the "star" school system in New Orleans, warning Negroes that a policy of coercive desegregation would enrage local whites and retard the development of black education.[18] Infuri-

16. After white Alabama voters defeated a proposed constitution in February, 1868, by boycotting the election, Congress enacted a "fourth reconstruction act" declaring a simple majority of votes cast sufficient to approve a constitution or ratify its results.

17. Ficklen, *History of Reconstruction in Louisiana*, p. 193.

18. New Orleans *Tribune*, Oct. 24, 30, 1867. I was unable to locate any extant copies of the *Republican* for this period.

ated by this turnabout, the *Tribune* denounced the Warmoth faction as "a white man's party" and accused it of betraying black interests after harvesting the black votes. Reminding readers of campaign promises for desegregated public schools, the *Tribune* charged, "they tell us that star schools are good enough for us, and we must not imagine that they will ever send THEIR children to school with negro children."[19] To prevent such double-dealing, the *Tribune* urged black delegates to vote as a bloc, demanding unequivocal guarantees of desegregated public schools in return for black votes on other issues.[20]

The convention, which began in Mechanics' Institute in New Orleans on November 23, was composed of three distinct factions. The Negro contingent, by far the largest with its forty-nine members, contained a few former slaves, but most of the black delegates had been free *gens de couleur*. The Negroes depended heavily upon the leadership of two men, one white and one black. Dr. George M. Wickcliffe, a white dentist from Clinton, had once edited an antiabolitionist journal but now embraced political and civil equality for Negroes with the zeal characteristic of a convert.[21] Pinckney Benton Stewart Pinchback, the bastard son of a white Mississippi planter and one of his slave women, had been freed by his father and sent north to study in a Cincinnati academy. During the Civil War he came to New Orleans as a cabin boy, then organized a company of black Union volunteers known as the Corps d'Afrique. Pinchback stayed in New Orleans, organized the fourth ward Republican club in 1867, became a member of the state central committee, and was elected to a seat in the convention, thus be-

---

19. *Ibid.*, Oct. 30, 1867.
20. *Ibid.*, Oct. 29, 1867.
21. See Ficklen, *History of Reconstruction in Louisiana*, p. 194. I incorrectly identified Wickliffe as a Negro in "A Pioneer Protest: The New Orleans Street-Car Controversy of 1867," *Journal of Negro History*, LIII (July, 1968), p. 231n.

ginning a career in public office that would make him the most powerful black politician in Louisiana for a generation.[22] To a man, the black delegates agreed with Wickliffe, Pinchback, and the *Tribune* that a constitution guaranteeing full political and civil rights to Negroes was the price the white Radicals must pay for their support.

This Negro strategy was categorically opposed by a group of sixteen native white Unionists representing the country parishes. Led by the pugnacious W. Jasper Blackburn, editor of the Homer *Iliad* and a delegate from Claiborne Parish, the sixteen were Republicans more because they opposed secession than because they loved Negroes. They believed that the blacks should be given full legal and political parity with whites, but they considered desegregation and other measures promoting "social equality" to be personally repugnant and politically suicidal. Unwilling to embrace the new egalitarianism, these so-called scalawags comprised an irreconcilable minority within the convention.

Between these two factions stood the white Radicals, a group of approximately thirty delegates. A few of them were native Louisianians, mostly New Orleanians who had been followers of Benjamin Flanders and A. P. Dostie during the occupation. Most of the white Radicals, however, were true carpetbaggers—men born in the North who came to Louisiana with the military or the Freedmen's Bureau and stayed on to develop political careers. Unlike the rural white Unionists and the Negroes, whose positions on racial issues were invariably determined by their beliefs, the white Radicals were guided less by ideological convictions than by pure political opportunism. They knew that Republican success required Negro support, but they also realized that they could develop a broader power base and gain greater indepen-

22. Richard A. Bardolph, *The Negro Vanguard* (New York, 1959), pp. 92–93; Agnes Smith Grosz, "The Political Career of Pinckney Benton Stewart Pinchback," *Louisiana Historical Quarterly*, XXVII (Apr., 1944), pp. 527–612. A critical biography of Pinchback is urgently needed.

dence from the blacks if they could attract a sizeable portion of the white vote. Accordingly, they planned to follow a course of compromise during the sessions, hoping to come up with a constitution that was egalitarian enough to assure the Negro vote but ambiguous enough to prevent total white disaffection.

The white Radicals learned the folly of such a scheme during the first week of debates, when Dr. Wickliffe proposed that all minor convention offices be divided equally between whites and Negroes. This suggestion set off an explosive dialogue. Whites charged that such a quota system would elevate color above merit. Blacks accused the whites of trying to keep power to themselves. Finally the scheme was rejected by a vote of forty-seven to thirty-eight, with Pinchback and a few other unity-minded Negroes voting in the negative.[23] The hostility evidenced during the debate, however, convinced white Radicals that they could not be all things to all men in racially polarized Louisiana. After that time they abandoned their quixotic search for native white support and concentrated upon enacting a constitution that would please the black majority.

Wickliffe wasted little time in putting his fellow white Radicals to the test. On November 30, as soon as the organizational business had been disposed of, the Clinton firebrand introduced a series of four resolutions on public education. The first stipulated that all children between the ages of six and eighteen be admitted to the public schools without racial qualification and added that there be "no schools established for any race." A second proposal enjoined municipalities from enacting or enforcing any local ordinances or regulations contrary to this open admissions policy. A third resolution authorized creation of a state university in New Orleans open to all qualified students. His final proposal demanded that all state-supported colleges, seminaries, and uni-

23. *Official Journal of the Proceedings of the Convention, for Framing a Constitution for the State of Louisiana* (New Orleans, 1867–1868), p. 4, cited hereafter as *Journal of the Convention, 1867–1868*; Ficklen, *History of Reconstruction in Louisiana*, pp. 194–95.

versities "be open in common to all classes of students, without distinction of race, color, or previous condition."[24]

The Wickliffe resolutions were sent to the committee on education, which reported its recommendations on December 12. The majority report, signed by six Negroes and one white, endorsed desegregation in all state-supported public schools and institutions of higher learning. A minority statement, signed by country-parish Unionists John L. Barrett, Peter Harper, G. Snider, and John Lynch, omitted all references to race.[25] On February 4, 1868, the committee presented its final recommendations, softened somewhat from the original Wickliffe proposals. The words "without distinction of race, color, or previous condition" were deleted from the article authorizing the state university in New Orleans, replaced by a rather vague admonition against regulations "violating the letter or spirit of the articles under this title." The proposal forbidding racial segregation in other state-supported colleges was abandoned altogether.[26]

Even so, the statement that became Article 135 in the final version of the constitution provided for the most ambitious attempt to bring about school desegregation tried in any southern state during the reconstruction era. The measure directed the legislature to establish at least one free public school, open to all children between the ages of six and twenty-one without racial qualification, in each parish. Moreover, the article specifically prohibited "separate schools or institutions of learning established exclusively for any race by the State of Louisiana."[27]

Opponents of the measure argued that such an approach was neither wise nor workable. W. L. McMillen warned that desegregation would "defeat the organization of a complete and thorough common school system in the State." W. Jasper Blackburn predicted that the proposal "will break up our free public

24. *Journal of the Convention*, 1867–1868, p. 17.
25. *Ibid.*, pp. 60–61.
26. *Ibid.*, p. 201.
27. *Ibid.*

school system, or at least virtually exclude the colored children from all participation therein." Imploring the delegates to follow a less controversial path, Blackburn argued, "I am a friend of all men, and more especially of all children, regardless of race or color; but I desire and aim to be so upon a safe and *practicable* basis." Other whites representing rural constituencies warned of the rampant fervor of white supremacist sentiment in the country parishes, but a coalition of Negroes and white Radicals ignored them, approving Article 135 by the overwhelming margin of sixty-one to twelve.[28]

Another prime black target was racial discrimination in places of public accommodation. Three days after Wickliffe introduced his resolutions on public education, R. I. Cromwell, a black delegate from New Orleans, complained that black people in Louisiana were consistently "proscribed and ostracised when entering into public places, or upon common carriers licensed and protected by this Constitution and laws of the State." He demanded a constitutional provision prohibiting such practices. On the next day, David Wilson, also from New Orleans, introduced a comprehensive measure banning segregation on public conveyances and affirming the legal right of every citizen of Louisiana to admission to "all amusements, drinking saloons, hotels, eating and lodging houses, billiard saloons, confectioneries, stores, shops, and all places where merchandise is sold; to asylums, colleges, churches, schools, hospitals, charitable institutions ... without regard to any distinction of race or color." A bizarre feature of the proposal was a rider stipulating that violators be fined not less than one thousand dollars and imprisoned for not less than one year. The fines, according to the rider, would be given to the

28. *Ibid.*, pp. 201, 275–77; Alexandria *Louisiana Democrat*, Mar. 18, Apr. 1, 1868; Monroe *Ouachita Telegraph*, Apr. 15, 1868; *Constitution Adopted by the State Constitutional Convention of the State of Louisiana, March 7, 1868* (New Orleans, 1868), p. 17, cited hereafter as *Constitution of 1868.*

aggrieved complainants. Wilson's measure was sent to the committee on the bill of rights, where it was wisely dropped.[29]

When the rights committee delivered its preliminary report on December 31, no mention was made of a provision to desegregate public accommodations. P. B. S. Pinchback suggested an article affirming "the right of all persons to travel on the common carriers and be entertained at all places of a public character in this State," which passed its first reading by a vote of sixty-seven to eight. Wickliffe, troubled that the measure was so vague that it might be circumvented by the courts, offered a substitute stating that all persons "shall enjoy equal rights and privileges, while traveling in this State; and all places of amusement, refreshments, entertainments of any public nature whatever, shall be open to all persons alike." As an additional guarantee against segregation, Wickliffe's proposal prohibited corporations, municipalities, and parishes from adopting or enforcing any "rules or regulations creating any distinction between persons on account of race, color or previous condition."[30]

After other suggestions had been offered, Pinchback introduced an amended version of his earlier measure. As its predecessor had done, this proposal guaranteed all persons "equal rights and privileges upon any conveyance of a public character; and all places of business or of public resort. . . ." Aware that past attempts to integrate such facilities had been overruled on the grounds that they had violated the sanctity of private property, Pinchback judiciously added a rider defining "places of a public character" as all businesses requiring a state, parish, or municipal license.[31] The measure did not please the conservative Unionists, three of whom condemned it as "subversive of all the rights of property and designed to force . . . an unjust and unnatural

29. *Journal of the Convention,* 1867–1868, pp. 27, 35.
30. *Ibid.,* p. 121.
31. *Ibid.,* pp. 122, 125; *Constitution of 1868,* p. 4.

equality."[32] But once again, the white Radicals joined with the Negroes to make the Pinchback proposal Article Thirteen of the new constitution by a vote of fifty-eight to sixteen.[33]

The articles banning segregated schools and public accommodations were the handiwork of the black delegates from origin to final passage. White Radical participation was more evident, however, in the adoption of a provision requiring all state office-holders to sign a statement endorsing the principle of racial equality. On January 28, Stephen B. Packard[34] introduced a measure forcing every state official to signify his willingness to "accept the civil and political equality of all men, and agree not to attempt to deprive any person or persons, on account of race, color, or previous condition, of any political or civil right, privilege, or immunity enjoyed by any other class of men. . . ."[35] Since Packard was at that time a close political ally of the men who controlled the antiintegrationist New Orleans *Republican*, it would appear that the purpose of the oath was to embarrass Democratic candidates and not to further the mixing of the races.[36] Packard's oath was roundly denounced by the conservatives from the country parishes. T. S. Crawford of Monroe castigated it as

32. Alexandria *Louisiana Democrat*, Mar. 18, 1868.

33. *Journal of the Convention,* 1867–1868, pp. 121–22, 125.

34. The only "carpetbagger" among the delegates to figure prominently in Republican politics in Louisiana after the convention, Packard later served as chairman of the state central committee, in which capacity he was instrumental in the ouster of Governor Henry C. Warmoth in 1872. In 1876 he was the Radical nominee for the governorship, but his disputed claims of victory were abandoned after the withdrawal of federal troops. See Ella Lonn, *Reconstruction in Louisiana after 1868* (New York, 1918), pp. 99–135, 406–94.

35. *Journal of the Convention,* 1867–1868, pp. 183–84, 260, 277.

36. Throughout the proceedings the white Radicals were more intent than the Negroes on disfranchising Confederate sympathizers. Several blacks, including Pinchback, voted against the harsh voter qualification provisions of Article Ninety-Nine. Pinchback and three other Negroes signed the constitution only after lodging a protest against the article, stating, "We are now, and ever have been, advocates of universal suffrage, it being one of the fundamental principles of the Radical Republican party." *Journal of the Convention,* 1867–1868, pp. 259, 293.

"absurd, disgraceful and ridiculous," and W. Jasper Blackburn complained that it was "irritating in verbiage while nothing is gained in principle."[37] Negro and white Radical votes, however, made the oath a part of Article 100 by a margin of forty-eight to sixteen.[38]

When the convention finished its work in March, 1868, it had drafted a document which had, at least theoretically, outlawed racial segregation in the public schools and places of public accommodation and had made a sworn belief in racial equality a qualification for public office. One student of nineteenth-century Louisiana life has written that the new code was "the product of many compromises, but followed essentially the recommendations of the white majority."[39] This interpretation is untenable. Four months before the convention began, the *Tribune* stated that the two paramount Negro goals were desegregated schools and access to public office.[40] Mainly because of the toughmindedness and unity of the black delegates, the new constitution went far beyond both demands. Negroes won not only desegregated schools, but mixed public travel and entertainment as well; they not only secured the right to vote and hold office, but the severe loyalty tests also assured them of a huge majority at the polls; they were not only guaranteed civil equality, but those who would deny it were also theoretically barred from public office. Coming after a century and a half of peonage and proscription, of slavery and segregation, the constitution of 1868 represented a monumental victory for the black people of Louisiana.

The new document confirmed the gravest fears of most white Louisianians, to whom white supremacy was perhaps as much an instinct as an ideology. It was unacceptable to many of the

37. *Ibid.*, pp. 260, 277.
38. *Ibid.*, p. 260.
39. Roger W. Shugg, *Origins of Class Struggle in Louisiana: A Social History of White Farmers and Laborers during Slavery and After, 1840–1875* (Baton Rouge, 1939), p. 221.
40. New Orleans *Tribune*, July 31, 1867.

conservative Unionist "scalawags" within the convention. Blackburn signed the constitution with reservations and returned to Claiborne Parish to fight for its ratification, but a number of his convention comrades did not follow his example. John T. Ludeling of Monroe, John L. Barrett of Union Parish, W. H. Cooley of Pointe Coupee Parish, Thomas P. Harrison of Lake Providence, T. S. Crawford of Monroe, and George W. Dearing, Jr., of Alexandria all refused to sign the document, then paraded their complaints across the pages of the Democratic press. Cooley, Harrison, and Dearing dismissed the equality oath as "an absurdity," warned that whites would never allow desegregated schools, and accused Article Thirteen of promoting "an unjust and unnatural equality."[41] Barrett and Ludeling cautioned that "mixed schools will not elevate the negroes, but will debase the whites."[42] Ludeling finally gave the constitution an eleventh-hour endorsement as the lesser of evils, but the other five "scalawags" joined in the Democratic campaign to defeat ratification.[43]

April 17 and 18, 1868, were the dates scheduled for elections to ratify or reject the constitution and to concurrently select an entire slate of legislators and state officials. The dual nature of the April elections forced the Democrats to make a difficult choice between running a ticket or concentrating upon defeating the constitution. Meeting in New Orleans in March, they decided to abandon the governorship and other state offices to the Radicals and devote their undivided attention to rejecting the despised constitution. To coordinate this campaign, they set up a state central committee, headed by Thomas L. Macon of New Orleans.[44] This strategy was endorsed warmly by the conservative press. The Monroe *Ouachita Telegraph* observed, "None but

41. Alexandria *Louisiana Democrat*, Mar. 18, 1868.
42. *Ibid.*, Apr. 1, 1868.
43. *Ibid.*, Mar. 18, Apr. 1, 1868; Monroe *Ouachita Telegraph*, Mar. 19, 1868.
44. Shreveport *South-Western*, Mar. 11, 1868; Monroe *Ouachita Telegraph*, Mar. 19, 1868; Alexandria *Louisiana Democrat*, Mar. 25, 1868; Baton Rouge *Tri-Weekly Advocate*, Apr. 1, 1868.

Radicals have any right to run for the offices under this Constitution; none but Radical Niggers and Nigger Radicals can dare to seek offices under it."[45] The Shreveport *South-Western* agreed that "to have introduced a scramble for office, in an election involving the status of the white race, would have been a sorry competition with carpet-baggers and free negroes for the loaves and fishes of office."[46]

The Republicans selected their slate of candidates in January. The gubernatorial nomination went to Henry Clay Warmoth, a Union officer from Illinois who had moved south with Grant, represented Louisiana briefly in the Congress in 1865, and helped found the New Orleans *Republican*, the unofficial voice of the white Radical faction, in the summer of 1867.[47] To balance the ticket racially, Oscar J. Dunn, a Negro who had run away from his owner and later purchased his freedom, was nominated for the lieutenant governorship.[48] Selected to run for the office of state superintendent of public education was Thomas W. Conway, a Baptist minister from New York who came to New Orleans as chaplain to a Negro army unit and later figured prominently in Freedmen's Bureau and Union League activities.[49] Rounding out the Republican slate were the militant G. M. Wickliffe for state auditor, Antoine Dubuclet for state treasurer, Simeon Belden for attorney general, and George E. Bovee for secretary of state.

A dissident Republican faction put up a partial ticket to oppose Warmoth and Conway. James G. Taliaferro, a native of Catahoula Parish who had presided over the constitutional convention, was nominated for the governorship, and J. W. McDonald, another rural "scalawag," was picked for the superintendency of education. Personalities apparently played a greater role

45. Monroe *Ouachita Telegraph*, Mar. 19, 1868.
46. Shreveport *South-Western*, Mar. 18, 1868.
47. Henry C. Warmoth, *War, Politics and Reconstruction: Stormy Days in Louisiana* (New York, 1930), pp. 5–27, 45–47.
48. Bardolph, *The Negro Vanguard*, p. 92.
49. Beasley, "History of Education in Louisiana," pp. 128–30.

in the schism than did ideology, for both tickets endorsed the constitution, soft-pedaled integration, and campaigned for the votes
of whites as well as blacks. Warmoth recalled sixty-two years
later that Taliaferro was a "Pure Radical" trying to "Africanize
the State" and that his own candidacy won the votes of "a large
number of conservative white men,"[50] but his memory was in-
correct. Taliaferro did not attract much black support, but he
did win faint-hearted endorsements from such Democratic newspapers as the New Orleans *Daily Picayune*, the Baton Rouge *Tri-
Weekly Advocate*, and the Shreveport *South-Western*.[51]

If the gubernatorial race was rather lackluster, the contest over
the "black and tan" constitution was anything but dull. The conservative press in the country parishes was extraordinarily abusive,
even by the unrestrained journalistic standards of the period.
The *Courier of the Teche* called the constitution "that wretched
abortion of party malignity" and accused it of "enormities and
crimes against reason, against religion and against nature." The
Shreveport *South-Western* labeled it a "mongrel monstrosity,"
and the neighboring *Caddo Gazette* described it as "a virtual re-
pudiation of every principle dear to the Caucasian race." The
Alexandria *Louisiana Democrat* denounced it for forcing a white
proprietor "to accept the patronage of any buck nigger that
chooses to walk into his store or shop." In perhaps the most imaginative passage of all, the Benton *Bossier Banner* portrayed the
constitution's creators as "social banditti, domestic bastards, cat-
amites, scallawags, slubberdegullions, cow-thieves, and jay-
hawkers."[52]

50. Warmoth, *War, Politics and Reconstruction*, pp. 51, 59.
51 New Orleans *Daily Picayune*, Apr. 10, 1868; Baton Rouge *Tri-
Weekly Advocate*, Apr. 15, 1868; Shreveport *South-Western*, Apr. 15,
1868.
52. Alexandria *Louisiana Democrat*, Apr. 8, 1868; Shreveport *South-
Western*, Mar. 11, Apr. 15, 1868; Monroe *Ouachita Telegraph*, Apr. 8,
1868; Benton *Bossier Banner*, Mar. 28, 1868.

The Democratic press in New Orleans was only slightly more restrained. The *Crescent* called the election "a question of liberty, of civilization, of social existence." The *Times* asked "whether this great State ... shall be Africanized." The *Picayune* wished blacks happiness "under their own vine and fig tree" but grimly warned the black man that "any effort to force his company on the white man ... will bring on him as bitter a curse as the Bible pronounces on his progenitor, Ham." The *Bee* described the constitution as "a condensed charter of all the turpitudes and monstrosities which negro depravity and fanatical partizanship are attempting to impose upon us" and concluded its campaign on election day by urging: "If you don't want your mothers and sisters, and wives and daughters insulted by insolent and depraved negro vagabonds.... If you are opposed to amalgamation and miscegenation, vote against the new constitution."[53]

But the flamboyant rhetoric was simply not enough to overcome the huge Negro registration majority. More than 90 percent of the registered whites turned out, giving Democratic candidates some impressive victories in the cities and the piney woods, where Negroes were a minority. They captured 16 of the 36 seats in the state senate and 45 of the 101 seats in the lower house. Whole Democratic slates swept to victories in Baton Rouge, Shreveport, and other cities. New Orleans voters gave the mayoralty and a majority of council seats to the Democrats. But victory in the main contests eluded them. The constitution was ratified by a vote of 51,737 to 39,076, mainly on the strength of enormous majorities in the bottomlands and the black neighborhoods of New Orleans and the other urban areas with substantial Negro populations. Warmoth outpolled Taliaferro for the governorship 64,941 to 38,046 and carried the rest of the regular

53. New Orleans *Daily Crescent*, Mar. 13, 1868; New Orleans *Times*, Apr. 17, 1868; New Orleans *Daily Picayune*, Mar. 10, 1868; New Orleans *Bee*, Mar. 27, Apr. 17, 1868.

Republican ticket to victory with him.[54] The black voters had spoken, and now the state had a Radical constitution to live by and a Radical administration to enforce the law. As a result, racial integration, hitherto inconceivable in the South and relatively untested anywhere in the United States, would have its day in Louisiana.

54. Ficklen, *History of Reconstruction in Louisiana*, pp. 201–3; Warmoth, *War, Politics and Reconstruction*, p. 59; Baton Rouge *Weekly Gazette and Comet*, Apr. 25, 1868; New Orleans *Bee*, Apr. 24, 1868.

FOUR

Politics and Public Accommodations
1868-77

The April elections brought the struggle over segregation into its second phase. The practice was now prohibited by law, but it continued to regulate interracial behavior in virtually every type of public activity throughout the state. The Radical Republicans now controlled the governorship and both houses of the general assembly. They could expect some support from a friendly federal government and, if necessary, from the occupational soldiers garrisoned in the state, but they needed to maintain the allegiance of the black voters to remain a viable political entity in Louisiana. To do this the Republicans would have to make an honest attempt to carry out their constitutional mandate to desegregate the schools and places of public accommodation, thus challenging the fervent prejudices of the "unreconstructed" white population.

Much of the responsibility rested with the new governor, Henry Clay Warmoth—by any standards one of the most enigmatic figures in the annals of southern politics. Born on May 9, 1842, in McLeansboro, Illinois, Warmoth became a self-taught lawyer at eighteen, a regimental commander at nineteen, a provost judge at twenty-two, a "territorial delegate" to Congress at twenty-three, and governor of Louisiana at twenty-six.[1] He was

1. Warmoth, *War, Politics and Reconstruction*, pp. 5–27, 45–47; Francis B. Harris, "Henry Clay Warmoth, Reconstruction Governor of Lou-

a man at odds with himself in many ways. He studied the Bible and pursued women with equal enthusiasm. He could be enthralled by grandiloquent lectures on the nobility of man yet grow rich on bribes and rebates because he understood so well man's baser capacities for greed and ambition.[2] An avid Unionist, he nevertheless identified strongly with the South and was given to recitations of his Virginia-Tennessee ancestry and boasts that he had "not a drop of any other than Southern blood" in his veins.[3] A creature of contradictions, Louisiana's *enfant terrible* was in many ways an ironically fitting symbol for the great conflicts raging in the state during the reconstruction.

In his approach to race relations, Warmoth represented the middle ground in the Republican coalition, for he was more liberal than such Louisiana-born segregationists as John T. Ludeling and W. Jasper Blackburn and far less egalitarian than northeasterners like Thomas W. Conway and E. S. Stoddard. In his campaign for the governorship, he strongly supported the new constitution but played down its integrationist provisions. As a founder of the New Orleans *Republican*, he undoubtedly endorsed its admonitions to impatient Negroes not to force the desegregation of the public schools. Opportunistic and somewhat naïve, Warmoth hoped to build a powerful political base in Louisiana by walking a tightrope between the interests of his black supporters and the fears and prejudices of potential white allies.

In his inaugural address, delivered before a joint session of the general assembly on July 13, 1868, Warmoth set the tenor of the

---

isiana," *Louisiana Historical Quarterly*, XXX (Apr., 1947), pp. 530–46; Richard N. Current, *Three Carpetbag Governors* (Baton Rouge, 1967), pp. 38–40.

2. To a great extent, Warmoth's evil reputation has been based upon allegations of extraordinary fiscal improprieties. Both Lonn, *Reconstruction in Louisiana*, and Harris, "Henry Clay Warmoth," leave the impression that Warmoth almost single-handedly corrupted a hitherto virtuous state. For a long overdue reappraisal, see the brief but excellent account in Current, *Three Carpetbag Governors*, pp. 59–64.

3. Warmoth, *War, Politics and Reconstruction*, p. 270.

racial strategy he hoped to pursue during his term in office. He pledged "equality before the law and the enjoyment of every political right of all the citizens of the State, regardless of race, color, or previous condition," but he also acknowledged that many Louisianians "not wanting in intelligence or virtue" could not accept that precept. Expressing faith in "the good sense, the discretion and inherent love of justice of the American people for the gradual wearing-away of the prejudices upon which alone this opposition is founded," Warmoth promised that his administration would chart a course "while resolute and manly . . . also moderate and discreet." He urged the legislators to act "as much as possible in harmony with the sentiments of the whole people" and warned them that he would prefer "that the course of legislation shall rather fall behind than outstrip the popular wishes and demands."[4]

Warmoth's blunt indications that he would rather not enforce the integrationist provisions of the new constitution brought grudging praise from many of the leading conservative newspapers. The New Orleans *Times*, commenting that "lip service is cheap," nevertheless lauded Warmoth's "determination to perform the duties of his office, not as a partisan, but as the chief magistrate of the State and people." The *Daily Crescent* praised Warmoth for "some wholesome convictions regarding the exigencies of the situation," and the New Orleans *Bulletin* expressed hope that the governor did not wish to experience "the exasperation of forcing social amalgamation in the schools or elsewhere."[5]

Warmoth's plea for a policy of "benign neglect" may have eased white anxieties, but it had no measurable effect on the newly elected black legislators. Louisiana Negroes had simply en-

4. *Official Journal of the Proceedings of the House of Representatives of the State of Louisiana, at the Session Begun and Held in New Orleans, June 29, 1868* (New Orleans, 1868), pp. 30–31, cited hereafter as *Journal of the House*, by year.

5. Warmoth, *War, Politics and Reconstruction*, pp. 62–63; New Orleans *Times*, July 14, 1868; New Orleans *Bulletin*, July 15, 1868.

dured too many generations of white oppression to have much faith in the "inherent love of justice of the American people." They had seen too many dramatic changes brought about by force to pin their hopes for equality on any "gradual wearing-away" of white prejudice. On past occasions when white Radicals had equivocated on the issue, black leaders had been able to bring them back in line by threatening to break ranks, taking most of the state's 82,907 black voters with them. This time they simply ignored Warmoth's admonitions.

On July 10, three days before the inaugural, Representative R. H. Isabelle, a black Republican from New Orleans, introduced a bill designed to enforce Article Thirteen by defining racial discrimination in places of public accommodation as a criminal offense. Stating that all persons "shall enjoy equal rights and privileges in their traveling, or being entertained, upon any conveyance of a public character, or place of public resort, or any place of business where a license is required by this State," the measure decreed that violators could be fined as much as five hundred dollars or jailed for as long as one year.[6]

The bill was referred to the house judiciary committee, which reported it favorably on August 24 by a vote of two to one. A minority opinion, written by Democrat James R. Currell of New Orleans, warned that the measure "would generate constant and serious turmoil in the community" and reminded the legislators of "the repugnance which the white population ... have to treating those of the colored race upon terms of social equality with themselves." Arguing that "laws cannot make society," Currell predicted that "even if it had the semblance of legality, such an enactment could never be enforced in the United States."[7] But the house passed the bill, fifty to fourteen, on August 28, and the senate concurred, fifteen to seven, on September 18.[8]

6. *Journal of the House*, 1868, p. 26.
7. *Ibid.*, pp. 157, 162.
8. *Ibid.*, pp. 172–74; *Official Journal of the Proceedings of the Senate of the State of Louisiana, at the Session Begun and Held in New Orleans,*

The measure was then sent to Governor Warmoth, presenting him with a dilemma of major proportions. He had been elected by black voters, and the strength of his administration rested heavily upon his rapport with the Negro legislators. But he was strongly opposed to a coercive campaign against segregation and obviously angered by the legislators' failure to act according to his inaugural exhortations. Moreover, Warmoth feared that the bill's passage could provoke widespread violence, for racial tensions were intensifying throughout the state. In the rural areas the bitterly contested presidential campaign was engendering daily acts of terrorism and intimidation.[9] On September 25 the shooting of a Negro by a white man brought New Orleans to the brink of a race riot. Fights erupted throughout the city. Some Negroes attacked a white grammar school, were driven back, then returned and fired several volleys into the building.[10] The school was hurriedly closed, averting further violence, but the incident was all Warmoth needed to convince himself that his signature on the Isabelle bill could precipitate a bloodbath. That afternoon he returned it unsigned to the legislature.[11]

In his veto message, the governor cited two specific objections to the measure. Its failure to adequately distinguish between intrastate and interstate carriers made it "impolitic and liable to produce unnecessary confusion and litigation." He also attacked as "not merely novel and unprecedented, but impracticable and pernicious" its definition of discrimination as a criminal act and not "a breach of obligations growing out of civil contracts." Hoping to forestall any attempts to amend the measure to skirt these specific objections, Warmoth added an emphatic reiteration of his hostility toward civil rights legislation in general. Con-

June 29, 1868 (New Orleans, 1868), pp. 183–84, cited hereafter as *Journal of the Senate*, by year.

9. Warmoth, *War, Politics and Reconstruction*, pp. 65–86; Ficklen, *History of Reconstruction in Louisiana*, pp. 210–31.

10. New Orleans *Bee*, Sept. 26, 1868.

11. *Journal of the House*, 1868, pp. 246–47.

demning such attempts "to force on those who differ from us our views of what is humane, or courteous, or Christianlike," he admonished the legislators that "forbearance and kindness, and the noble belief in the brotherhood of man, must spring from a higher source than the fear of punishment. They can never be forced to grow by pains and penalties."[12]

The veto marked the first definite step in Warmoth's enigmatic progression from Radical Republicanism to fusion with elements of the white conservative opposition. Segregationist newspapers hailed the move as "an earnest of other any further movements which will, we hope, tend to the good."[13] Within the Radical camp, the reaction was predictably angry. Oscar J. Dunn, Warmoth's moderate black lieutenant governor, later cited the veto as the beginning of the break between the two men.[14] Judge Henry C. Dibble recalled that "all the opposition to Governor Warmoth among the republicans of the State began when he refused to sign . . . the first social equality bill."[15]

The reaction was particularly vehement among the black lawmakers. R. H. Isabelle responded to the veto with an impassioned outburst against discrimination, singling out for special condemnation the governor, swarthy Mexicans who were treated as whites, and some dark-skinned Portuguese vendors who refused to serve Negroes at their coffee stands in New Orleans. Reminding his colleagues that the blacks had been promised "all the rights and privileges of the white man," Isabelle warned "that the negro must strike while the iron was hot." Representative Murrell of Lafourche Parish noted some of Warmoth's campaign commitments and surmised that the governor had been "tight" at the time. George Washington of Assumption Parish accused Warmoth of being "weak kneed" and "afraid of Sicilian assassins,"

12. *Ibid.*

13. New Orleans *Daily Picayune*, Sept. 29, 1868; see also New Orleans *Bee*, Sept. 27, 1868, and Plaquemines *Iberville South*, Oct. 3, 1868.

14. Harris, "Henry Clay Warmoth," p. 557.

15. Quoted in *ibid.*

urged the legislature to impeach the governor, and warned white supremacists that Negroes were ready to fight for their rights.[16]

Despite their outrage the Isabelle bill was dead, for the governor could depend upon the votes of a few white Republicans and every Democrat to sustain the veto.[17] Rather than suffer a certain humiliating defeat, black strategists decided to submit another measure written to avoid Warmoth's specific objections to its predecessor. On September 28 Representative Dennis Burrell, a Negro from St. John the Baptist Parish, introduced a bill entitled "An Act to Enforce the Provisions of the Thirteenth Article of the Constitution of Louisiana." This proposal simply reiterated Article Thirteen, stated that victims of discrimination could seek redress by civil suits, and decreed that such actions be given preferential scheduling on court dockets. A rather weak piece of legislation, vague and toothless, it attracted little support and died quietly in the house judiciary committee.[18]

On January 12, 1869, State Senator Pinchback, creator of Article Thirteen, introduced into the senate a bill entitled "An Act to Enforce the Thirteenth Article of the Constitution of This State, and to Regulate the Licenses Mentioned in the Said Thirteenth Article." Carefully setting acceptable guidelines for the right to refuse service, the Pinchback bill granted common carriers and businesses the right to refuse admission for nonpayment and the right to eject patrons for "gross, vulgar or disorderly conduct, or ... any act tending to injure the business," provided that such policies "make no distinction on account of race or color." The bill required all future licenses issued by the state, parishes, and municipalities to contain the express condition that "the place of business or public resort shall be open to the accommodation and patronage of all persons without distinction or discrimination on account of race or color." Injured parties were

16. New Orleans *Bee*, Sept. 27, 1868; New Orleans *Daily Picayune*, Sept. 27, 1868; Monroe *Ouachita Telegraph*, Oct. 7, 1868.
17. New Orleans *Daily Picayune*, Sept. 29, 1868.
18. *Journal of the House*, 1868, p. 248.

given the right to sue violators for "exemplary as well as actual" damages in civil actions, and the state was empowered to revoke the licenses of guilty businesses. The bill won senate approval on February 8 by a margin of twenty to nine, was endorsed by the house a few days later, and was sent on to a most reluctant Governor Warmoth.[19]

The Democratic press, aware from past experience that Warmoth was conspicuously vulnerable to pressure, conducted a fierce campaign against the legislation. The New Orleans *Bee* predicted that it would be "impossible to enforce, and ... can produce nothing but strife and ill-blood." The New Orleans *Commercial Bulletin* claimed that a Negro "may be able to obtain a ticket of admission, but no New Orleans audience will ever permit him to take his seat except in the places allotted for colored persons." The New Orleans *Daily Crescent* mournfully prophesied that "the social anarchy resulting from this policy ... would shatter the very basis of trade and plunge the city into an abyss of commercial disaster and decay from which it would never emerge."[20]

This conservative pressure was countered by the return of the New Orleans *Tribune*. Closed down in April, 1868, because of financial difficulties, the *Tribune* was resurrected by publishers Louis and J. B. Roudanez in January, 1869, to assist in the struggle for a public accommodations bill. In issue after issue the "odious and unjust restrictions" of the color line were denounced as "un-American, un-republican, un-democratic, un-reasonable, and un-Christian." Portraying the Pinchback bill as a symbolic blow against all racial injustice, the *Tribune* urged Negroes to unite and "throw off a tremendous load which has been our inheritance for centuries."[21]

For nearly two weeks the governor agonized over his options.

19. *Journal of the Senate*, 1869, pp. 21, 98, 159.
20. New Orleans *Bee*, Feb. 7, 1869; New Orleans *Daily Crescent*, Jan. 12, 1869; Lonn, *Reconstruction in Louisiana*, p. 41.
21. New Orleans *Tribune*, Feb. 4, 1869.

He did not want to sign the bill, thus adding to his growing list of administrative and political problems, but he could not come up with a plausible reason for not doing so. He could not veto it on constitutional grounds, for it conformed precisely to the guidelines on redress he had proposed only five months before. He could not convincingly discard it in the interests of tranquility, for racial tensions had diminished considerably since the November elections. Moreover, his flirtation with the white conservatives had brought no tangible results, and he had little reason to believe that a second veto would bear more fruit than the first had done. On the other hand, Warmoth realized that another rebuff could well shatter his increasingly fragile political base by driving black Republican leaders into irreconcilable opposition. The *Tribune* was berating him as "unfaithful to the principles upon which he was elected."[22] His first veto had cost him the support of Oscar J. Dunn; a second would alienate others, including the powerful Pinchback. Taking the course of least resistance, the governor reluctantly added his signature to the measure on February 23.[23]

Once written into law, the Civil Rights Act of 1869 did little to end racial discrimination in places of public accommodation. Two weeks after its enactment, the failure of Negroes to test its provisions prompted the New Orleans *Daily Picayune* to dismiss the legislation as a "dead letter." In his autobiography, Warmoth recalled that the law was not enforced because "the colored people were too wise to undertake to force themselves upon white people who did not want them."[24]

The governor's memory was not completely accurate. On one occasion the law was tested in the courts and enforced. In January, 1871, C. S. Sauvinet, the black civil sheriff of Orleans Parish, attempted to buy a drink in the Bank Saloon at 6 Royal Street.

22. *Ibid.*, Jan. 7, 1869.
23. *Journal of the Senate*, 1869, p. 159.
24. New Orleans *Daily Picayune*, Mar. 6, 1869; Warmoth, *War, Politics and Reconstruction*, p. 92.

Proprietor J. A. Walker refused to serve the lawman and demanded that he leave the tavern. Sauvinet filed suit in Eighth District Court on January 27, demanding $10,000 in damages and cancellation of Walker's liquor license. Three months later District Judge Henry C. Dibble handed down his verdict. Walker was allowed to retain his license but was forced to pay Sauvinet $1,000 in exemplary damages plus all legal costs on the grounds that Sauvinet's "citizenship has been degraded. He should have exemplary damages." Dibble justified the large settlement by ruling that the penalty "should be estimated as will sanctify the principle involved and deter others from inflicting the same injury."[25]

Although Dibble's verdict was condemned by one New Orleans white supremacist as "a judgement which . . . shocked the consciences,"[26] it apparently did little to shock other blacks into similar lawsuits. More typical was the case of State Senator Butler, a Negro from Plaquemines Parish, who occupied a seat in the cabin of the steamboat *Bannock City*, an accommodation reserved exclusively for white passengers. Butler was told by a steward "that he was not in his proper place, that he must leave the cabin and go out on the guards." When Butler refused to do so, he was seized by several white passengers, beaten with an iron bar, and thrown out onto the deck.[27] Despite Butler's political position and the obvious liability of the *Bannock City* for the civil rights violation and assault charges, nothing came of the incident.

Despite the Civil Rights Act of 1869 and the Dibble verdict in the Sauvinet case, the color line in places of public accommodation remained virtually unchallenged. In May, 1871, the Baton Rouge *Grand Era*, a short-lived Negro newspaper, demanded "the right to travel on any public conveyance in accordance with

25. New Orleans *Republican*, Jan. 28, Apr. 28, 1871.
26. Daniel Warren Brickell to the New Orleans *Times*, Mar. 25, 1872, in the Daniel Brickell Papers, Louisiana State University Archives.
27. New Orleans *Republican*, Mar. 23, 1871.

the class of tickets purchased; the right to appear in public assemblies and places of amusement."[28] In December, 1872, nearly four years after adoption of the 1869 law, a number of black state legislators attested to its failure during a debate over pending federal civil rights legislation. According to one black lawmaker, it was "very hard that a Chinman [*sic*] has rights which were denied to native American colored men." Another testified that whenever he rode on a steamboat, "however unexceptionable his behavior, he was denied the comforts of traveling accorded to all other people." A third bitterly assailed the railroad practice of compelling black passengers to ride in old box-cars "with dogs and dead hogs."[29]

Although many factors were responsible for its weakness, the essential drawback of the Pinchback law was its emphasis on civil litigation. Most Louisiana Negroes were poorly informed on the complexities of civil law, and few could afford the services of a competent attorney for protracted judicial proceedings. Its failure to bring an end to discrimination prompted black legislators to attempt to secure new and more effective civil rights legislation. On January 26, 1870, R. H. Isabelle introduced "An Act Forbidding Unjust Discrimination on Account of Color or Race and Providing Means for Enforcing the Same." The measure prohibited racial segregation on common carriers and in licensed places of public accommodation. Like his ill-fated 1868 rights bill, Isabelle's new proposal defined violation as a criminal act and provided mandatory penalties. Lawbreakers would be fined from ten to fifty dollars for each infraction, and their businesses could be closed down until compliance was guaranteed. An unusual and somewhat questionable feature of the bill was a provision that cases were to be tried by local justices of the peace and parish recorders, a ploy aimed at steering them away from the

28. Quoted in *ibid*, May 11, 1871.
29. New Orleans *Daily Picayune*, Dec. 21, 31, 1872.

jurisdiction of judges appointed by the governor. The house approved the measure on March 9, and the senate voted its assent three days later.[30]

The second Isabelle bill once again placed Governor Warmoth in a delicate position. He did not accept as constitutional the scheme delegating jurisdiction to justices of the peace. Moreover, his implacable opposition to criminal prosecution of civil rights violations was a matter of public record, and to surrender openly on that point would subject him to unavoidable humiliation. He also realized that he would reap no great political benefits if he signed the bill, for his endorsement of the 1869 measure had done little to heal his rift with the black lawmakers. The irony of his position, however, was that he stood to gain no more by rejecting the bill. Both parties were preparing for crucial congressional and legislative elections in the fall, and a veto would almost certainly tear the fragile Republican coalition apart. Politically vulnerable either way, Warmoth resorted to a rather clever stratagem. He held the bill on his desk for nearly nine months, postponing the inevitable confrontation until the 1870 elections were safely out of the way. Then, on January 2, 1871, on the opening day of the new legislative session, he vetoed it and sent it back to the house.

In his veto message, Warmoth argued that the bill was patently unconstitutional on several counts. He pointed out that parish recorders were not legally authorized to handle criminal cases. He noted that a defendant's right to trial by jury would be necessarily abridged, for under Louisiana law justices of the peace did not have the authority to impanel jurors. He reiterated his opinion that discrimination imposed by individuals or corporations should be contested by civil litigation, not criminal proceedings. Noting that the Civil Rights Act of 1869 was still in force, he advised the legislators that "until at least some well di-

30. *Journal of the House,* 1870, pp. 106, 327; *Journal of the Senate,* 1870, p. 327; 1871, p. 4.

rected effort has been made, through the proper courts, to enforce its provisions, and they have been proven defective or inoperative, further legislation in this direction is unnecessary."[31]

Warmoth's decision may have been judicially sound, but it was politically suicidal. He was already at odds over patronage and control of the party machinery with the so-called "Custom-House Gang," a group of northern-born Radicals led by U.S. Senator William Pitt Kellogg and Central Committee Chairman Stephen B. Packard. In January, 1871, Warmoth's opposition to the senatorial ambitions of James F. Casey, a brother-in-law of President Grant, drove the dissidents into open rebellion.[32] Almost simultaneously, his rejection of the Isabelle bill earned him the implacable enmity of nearly every influential black politician in Louisiana. Warmoth later charged that some unnamed "white and colored Radical politicians" had concocted the bill as part of a conspiracy "to consolidate the whole colored race" against him.[33] Whatever the motivations behind the measure, his assessment of the result was substantially correct. He soon became something of a political anachronism, an incumbent governor without a party organization or a popular following.

The Radicals split openly in August, 1871, into factions headed by Warmoth and Packard, each stridently claiming recognition as the legitimate Republican organization in the state. After six months of acrimonious bickering and maneuvering, complete with bribery and mobs and finally rival police forces, rump conventions, and legislatures, Warmoth managed to maintain control of the Republican party machinery, but in the process he alienated even more elements within the organization. Finally realizing the hopelessness of his position, Warmoth abandoned the party he had led to power in Louisiana and entered into a rather bizarre alliance with the Democrats to prevent the "Cus-

31. *Journal of the Senate*, 1871, pp. 4–6.
32. Lonn, *Reconstruction in Louisiana*, pp. 76–77.
33. Warmoth, *War, Politics and Reconstruction*, p. 92.

tom-House" Radicals from capturing control of the state government in the elections scheduled for November 4, 1872. The
"fusion" forces put together a ticket headed by gubernatorial
candidate John McEnery, a Democrat, and a legislative slate made
up of Democrats and Warmoth Republicans. The Radicals nominated Senator Kellogg for the governorship and C. C. Antoine,
a Negro, for lieutenant governor. After a contested election and
a brief period of dual governments, a Republican returning board
decided in favor of Kellogg and Antoine, prolonging reconstruction in Louisiana for four more years.[34]

These political realignments brought striking shifts in the racial
approaches adopted by the various factions. Up to the elections
of 1872, Republicans and Democrats had divided unequivocally
on the race question, with Radicals championing Negro suffrage
and civil rights and Democrats proclaiming unyielding devotion
to the tenets of white supremacy. But the obvious importance of
the Negro vote in 1872 temporarily obscured traditional racial
doctrines. The Kellogg forces successfully garnered most of the
black vote with an integrated ticket running on a platform which
endorsed the desegregation of public schools and accommodations. The fusion coalition made a bid for black support by including a token Negro on their ticket[35] and by writing into their
platform the resolution "That we recognize the political and
civil rights of all men, and pledge ourselves to maintain them."[36]
A short-lived "reform" faction, a New Orleans-centered, busi-
nessman-oriented crusade for fiscal integrity instigated by Isaac
N. Marks and William M. Randolph, vied openly for black support by inviting Negroes to their rallies, espousing interracial
amity, and promising to uphold the legal and civil rights accorded
Negroes by Louisiana law.[37]

34. Lonn, *Reconstruction in Louisiana*, pp. 73–229; Charles L. Dufour,
"The Age of Warmoth," *Louisiana History*, VI (Fall, 1965), pp. 351–63.
35. Samuel Armstead, candidate for secretary of state.
36. Quoted in Current, *Three Carpetbag Governors*, pp. 55–56.
37. T. Harry Williams, "The Louisiana Unification Movement of

Although the reform group's vision of restoring honest government through interracial cooperation foundered on the rocks of white elitism and black suspicion, the basic idea survived in the minds of its creators. In the spring of 1873, Marks and others began to plan what one historian has described as "one gigantic political organization that, sweeping everything before it, would gain control of the state government and restore harmony and stability."[38] In June, 1873, a "committee of one hundred" eminent New Orleanians, fifty whites and fifty blacks, began to formulate a platform enunciating the group's reform objectives and setting forth the program for Negro civil rights they planned to pursue.

The drafting of this manifesto was entrusted to a smaller group of five whites and five blacks headed by New Orleans's most venerated war hero, General G. T. Beauregard, then president of the New Orleans and Carollton Railroad. The commercial orientation of the Unification movement was amply demonstrated by the white members of the committee. James I. Day was president of an insurance company and a former bank president. Auguste Bohn was a bank president and director of an insurance company and the New Orleans Cotton Exchange. Judge William Randolph was a prominent attorney. Isaac Marks, the ideological instigator of Unification, was a South Carolina Jew who had migrated to New Orleans around 1836, had been a leading Union Whig, and was currently president of one insurance company, a director of another, and owner of a large grocery. The five Negroes on the committee were Charles H. Thompson, a minister and school board member; Louis C. Roudanez, Paris-educated editor of the defunct New Orleans *Tribune;* philanthropist Aristide Mary; State Senator George Y. Kelso, a former Warmoth floor leader; and Lieutenant Governor C. C. Antoine, a leader in the Custom-

1873," *Journal of Southern History*, XI (Aug., 1945), p. 351; Lonn, *Reconstruction in Louisiana*, pp. 140–41; Warmoth, *War, Politics and Reconstruction*, p. 178.

38. Williams, "Louisiana Unification Movement," p. 350.

House Radical faction that was the prime target of the Unification forces.[39]

A truly remarkable document, the Unification movement's platform certainly represented the high-water mark of cooperation between native whites and Negroes during the reconstruction period in Louisiana. It explained the state's "dire extremity" as the "fruit of unnatural division" between the races. It endorsed "the equal and impartial exercise by every citizen of Louisiana of every civil and political right guaranteed by the constitution & laws of Louisiana, by the constitution & laws of the U.S. & by the laws of Honor, Brotherhood & fair dealing." Specifically, it offered Negroes an equal distribution of political offices and advocated desegregated public schools, factories, places of public accommodation, and common carriers. Urging "the rapid removal of all prejudices heretofore existing against the colored citizens of Louisiana," it appealed to all Louisianians to "join and cooperate with us in erecting this monument to unity, concord & justice and like ourselves forever bury beneath it all past prejudices on the subject of race or color."[40]

The motives of the white sponsors were mixed. Marks, a genuine racial egalitarian, once went on record as stating: "It is my determination to continue to battle against these abstract, absurd and stupid prejudices, and to bring to bear the whole force of my character . . . to break them down. They must disappear; *they will disappear.*"[41] But others, like General Beauregard, were more pragmatic. In a speech delivered in New Orleans in July, 1873, the "great Creole" told his audience that "nothing but the forbearance of the colored people prevents them from subjecting common carriers, and all keepers of places of public resort, to such losses and annoyances as would speedily compel the practical acknowledgement of their rights or the abandonment of

39. *Ibid.*, pp. 356–58.
40. "Unification Platform," original draft in the Unification Papers, Louisiana State University Archives.
41. Quoted in Williams, "Louisiana Unification Movement," p. 362.

business."[42] If Negro rights were already there for the taking, Beauregard reasoned that white recognition of those rights was a very small price to pay for black assistance in overthrowing the Radical Republicans.

An interracial crusade to restore home rule and assure Negro rights may have been a compelling ideal, but it was a patently unrealistic rationale on which to build a political organization. It must be understood that reconstruction in Louisiana was much less a tug-of-war between Republicans and Democrats than it was a struggle between Negroes and whites to determine whether racial equality or white supremacy would be the guiding philosophy behind public policies. More than the possibility of a Democratic restoration would be required to induce most whites to swallow an open endorsement of black equality in places of public accommodation; more than a pious pledge of brotherhood would be needed to persuade Negroes to forsake the party of Abraham Lincoln and unite with their old owners and oppressors. Inevitably, the hopes of the Unification movement were dashed upon the rocks of mutual mistrust.

White conservatives throughout rural Louisiana abhorred the plan. Unlike New Orleans whites, they had for the most part been able to avoid Radical interference in their day-to-day affairs. Given the choice, most rural whites plainly preferred the irritation of a Republican administration in New Orleans to the odious humiliation of accepting their former slaves as social equals. The Monroe *Ouachita Telegraph* loathed "in every fibre of our being" this alliance built "on the basis of perfect equality of whites and blacks."[43] The Shreveport *Times* proclaimed that "the battle between the races for supremacy ... must be fought out here ... boldly and squarely; the issue cannot be satisfactorily adjusted by a repulsive commingling of antagonistic races."[44] With rural

42. G. T. Beauregard, *The Unification Question: Address of General G. T. Beauregard to the People of Louisiana* (New Orleans, 1873), p. 2.
43. Monroe *Ouachita Telegraph*, June 21, 1873.
44. Quoted in Williams, "Louisiana Unification Movement," p. 363.

bigotry ruling out any chance for acceptance in the country parishes, Unification remained purely a New Orleans phenomenon.

Even in the city, the movement could not overcome the suspicions nurtured for generations. At a rally staged on July 15, under a huge banner proclaiming "Equal Rights—One Flag—One Country—One People," Unification foundered. State Senator J. Henri Burch, a black Kellogg Radical foolishly selected as a speaker, sabotaged the movement by condescendingly congratulating the whites for abandoning their silly prejudices. Burch further enraged whites with the disclosure that Negroes would support Unification only after the whites had transformed all their promises into accomplishments.[45] Even more disastrous was a pledge signed by Roudanez, Mary, Antoine, and other influential black members of the "committee of one hundred" that they would participate wholeheartedly in the campaign to secure home rule "as soon as the existing opposition against the enjoyment of our rights . . . shall have ceased."[46] Although the Negroes can hardly be blamed for their misgivings, their action shattered the fragile coalition. Within days of the unfortunate rally, Unification was dead, agitation for civil rights was once again a Republican monopoly, and urban and rural Democrats were once more uniting around their traditional advocacy of white supremacy in Louisiana politics and society.[47]

The Radicals had not been idle while their Unification adversaries had been trying to entice away their black supporters. In early February, 1873, a bill entitled "An Act to Protect the Civil Rights of Citizens, Declaring Certain Forfeitures for Acts in Derogation of Such Rights and Directing Proceedings to That End, Making Certain Acts in Violation of Civil Rights a Misdemeanor

45. *Ibid.*, p. 365.
46. "Pledge," undated, in the Unification Papers, Louisiana State University Archives.
47. Williams, "Louisiana Unification Movement," p. 367.

and Declaring the Punishment Therefore" guaranteed all citizens "equal and impartial accommodations, advantages, facilities and privileges" on all common carriers and places of public business. Like the Civil Rights Act of 1869, it provided for revocation of licenses and recourse to civil suits. A novel feature of the new bill, however, was its attempt to regulate interstate carriers. Forbidding interstate carriers operating on Louisiana soil or waters from adopting or enforcing "any rule or regulation discriminating against any citizen of this State on account of race or color," the measure made violation a misdemeanor and stated that convicted personnel would "be fined or imprisoned at the discretion of the court, or both." Moreover, the bill authorized the state attorney general to personally prosecute civil suits for damages on behalf of alleged victims.[48]

The bill predictably aroused outraged opposition in the legislature, but the Radical returning board that certified Kellogg's claim to the governorship had also awarded a large number of disputed seats to the Republican candidates. As a result the measure won senate approval on February 27 and secured an overwhelming house endorsement on the same day.[49] With its provisions for criminal prosecution and regulation of interstate carriers, the bill went far beyond the limits imposed for four years by Henry C. Warmoth. But Warmoth was no longer the state's chief executive, and William Pitt Kellogg, his successor, was a vastly different man. Unlike Warmoth, Kellogg entertained no illusions that he could please all of the people of Louisiana. He knew that Negro voters had put him in office and that a Republican returning board had certified the verdict. Warmoth's refusal to accept desegregation by decree had been a major factor in his political downfall, and the lesson was not lost upon his successor. Overlooking the questionable constitutionality of the bill's inter-

48. *Acts of Louisiana*, 1873, no. 84, pp. 156–57.
49. *Journal of the House*, 1873, pp. 193–94.

state commerce provision, Kellogg signed it into law on April 19, 1873.[50] In his annual message for 1874, he stated that "all has been done that can be done" in the way of legislation, called for the strict enforcement of existing laws, and promised that toward that end "the executive will do his whole duty."[51]

The Civil Rights Act of 1873 was never put to the legal test. A lawsuit in 1875 challenging steamboat segregation on the Mississippi River sought redress under the less controversial 1869 act, despite its significantly weaker provisions.[52] But the inadequacies of both state laws became irrelevant on March 1, 1875, when President Grant signed into law the federal Civil Rights Act of 1875. As proposed originally by Senator Charles Sumner of Massachusetts in May, 1870, the measure prohibited racial segregation in cemeteries, public schools, inns, theatres, public transportation, and all other places of public accommodation and amusement. Northern critics, rather sensitive over local segregation practices, forced deletion of cemeteries and public schools from the final version. Even so, the Sumner Act was strong legislation. Upon conviction, violators could be fined from five hundred to one thousand dollars, jailed for a period of not less than thirty days, and forced to pay the injured party the sum of five hundred dollars in damages.[53]

Reactions to the act in Louisiana were mixed. The New Orleans *Daily Picayune* reported that Negro leaders seemed indifferent, but observed that "the general herd of blacks" regarded it as a "second emancipation proclamation, by which they are to gain some sort of indefinite privileges which they suppose the whites to enjoy."[54] The Opelousas *Courier* summed up the feelings of many rural whites when it intimated that the measure

50. *Acts of Louisiana*, 1873, p. 157.
51. *Journal of the Senate*, 1874, pp. 15–16.
52. See *Hall v. De Cuir*, 95 U.S. 485 (1878).
53. An excellent account of the struggle to enact this bill can be found in Milton R. Konvitz and Theodore Leskes, *A Century of Civil Rights* (New York, 1961), pp. 91–93.
54. New Orleans *Daily Picayune*, Mar. 6, 1875.

violated divine decree.[55] In New Orleans there was little initial excitement. The *Picayune* reasoned that if Negroes "were disposed to press the matter, the State laws afford them every facility to be found in the act of Congress."[56] This state of apparent calm prompted the New Orleans *Times* to dismiss the bill as "having by general consent been quietly ignored by all parties."[57]

The epitaph was somewhat premature. On the evening of March 9 two black politicians, State Senator T. B. Stamps of Jefferson Parish and Sixth District Assessor Dejoie, successfully gained entry into the white section of the St. Charles Theatre to see the play *Sir Giles Overreach*. A white exodus resulted, but the two Negroes were not disturbed.[58] The New Orleans *Bulletin* interpreted the incident as a surrender of tragic proportions, lamenting that the "issue has been made and the point yielded, that at least one of our theatres will hereafter be open to negroes, in common with those whites who are inclined to attend."[59] The *Times* called the deed "a gratuitous insult" to the Negro community, reasoning that refusal to occupy seats in the "nigger heaven" was tantamount to a rejection of the culprits' African heritage.[60]

Despite rumors circulating about the city that mass attempts to desegregate other theatres would take place, none followed the Stamps-Dejoie escapade.[61] More common were incidents in white saloons. Already the target of a successful lawsuit in 1871, many New Orleans taverns apparently altered their old policy of directly refusing service to Negroes. A few tried to separate the races by serving blacks in one room and whites in another. In one such saloon, owned by Jacinto Labrenna at the corner of Robin and Peters, a Negro refused service in the white room re-

55. Opelousas *Courier*, Mar. 20, 1875.
56. New Orleans *Daily Picayune*, Mar. 7, 1875.
57. New Orleans *Times*, Mar. 9, 1875.
58. New Orleans *Daily Picayune*, Mar. 10, 1875.
59. New Orleans *Bulletin*, Mar. 10, 1875.
60. New Orleans *Times*, Mar. 10, 1875.
61. New Orleans *Bee*, Mar. 10, 1875.

turned with two friends and again demanded drinks in the white area. After being rejected again by manager Mike Larkin, the trio waited until darkness had set in, returned, and set fire to the tavern.[62]

Unable or unwilling to challenge state and federal laws by directly refusing to serve Negroes in places of public resort, white proprietors devised ingenious ways to circumvent the law. When two Negroes attempted to purchase tickets to a show at the Varieties Theatre on the corner of Royal and Conti, Mr. Hippler, the manager, told them that admission was free but required the purchase of a $2.50 "beer ticket." Unable to pay the exorbitant fee, the pair departed.[63] Saloons often served persistent Negroes but doctored the drinks to make them unpalatable. At George McCloskey's saloon at 76 St. Charles a Negro asked for a soft drink and was given one loaded with cayenne pepper. The angry black tried to have McCloskey arrested, but the policeman, according to the *Times*, considered the dispute "entirely a matter of taste."[64] At brother Hugh McCloskey's tavern on Canal Street three Negroes were served soft drinks nearly bereft of syrup, leading to a minor donnybrook.[65]

Gradually, tests of the Sumner law subsided. In a few instances Negroes were able to demand and receive service in white facilities until the abdication of the Radicals in 1877, but these were striking exceptions to the rule. Tests of the Civil Rights Act of 1875 were virtually nonexistent in smaller towns and in the rural areas, where black timidity, the "shotgun sovereignty" of local whites, and the weakness of state and federal authority rendered the certain consequences more imposing than the dubious gains could offset. Even in New Orleans, where conditions were much more propitious, such impediments as sabotaged service and the expensive, drawn-out process of legal recourse prevented more

62. New Orleans *Daily Picayune*, Mar. 23, 1875.
63. *Ibid.*, Mar. 6, 1875.
64. New Orleans *Times*, Mar. 23, 1875.
65. New Orleans *Daily Picayune*, Mar. 23, 1875.

than token attempts to desegregate places of public accommodation.

State institutions, the public facilities most directly under Republican control, were not affected to a great extent by the struggle over segregation during the period. In many instances, it is virtually impossible to determine racial arrangements, for official reports often ignored them to avoid possible displeasure. A state school for the blind was established in Baton Rouge in 1871. The bill chartering the institution expressly prohibited policies "so as to deprive any person on account of race or color the privilege of admission," but in practice only whites were accepted.[66]

The Charity Hospital in New Orleans had been segregated before the Civil War, but one of the first steps taken by the new Republican board of administrators at its meeting on September 7, 1868, was the adoption of a resolution to the effect that "in admitting sick persons to the benefits of this Hospital no distinction be made founded on race, color, or previous condition."[67] It is not known if this directive was applied to the wards, as the official reports scrupulously avoided racial statistics throughout the period. It is probable, however, that ward segregation was maintained, for the reports submitted shortly after the Radical collapse indicate the existence of systematic ward-by-ward racial separation.[68] The Charity Hospital in Shreveport was chartered by the legislature in 1876 by a bill prohibiting racial discrimination in the facility, but it had barely begun to function before the restoration of Democratic rule.[69]

66. *Acts of Louisiana*, 1871, no. 92, pp. 208–10; *First Annual Report of the Officers and Trustees of the Louisiana Institution for the Education of the Blind, and the Industrial Home for the Blind, to the General Assembly of the State of Louisiana, for the Year Ending December 31, 1873* (New Orleans, 1874), p. 7; *Eighth Report . . . for the Years 1880 and 1881* (Baton Rouge, 1882), p. 11.

67. *Report of the Board of Administrators of the Charity Hospital at New Orleans to the Legislature of the State of Louisiana* (New Orleans, 1868), p. 8, cited hereafter as *Report, Charity Hospital*, by year.

68. *Ibid.*, 1880, p. 7.

69. *Acts of Louisiana*, 1876, no. 40, pp. 77–78.

Although official reports from the Louisiana State Penitentiary in Baton Rouge avoided racial designations, white and black inmates were quartered separately. According to a report published in 1874 in the New Orleans *Republican*, the Negroes were not only segregated, they were given more arduous work details, more brutal punishment for infractions, and fewer blankets than white convicts.[70] Jailhouse segregation prevailed in local lockups as well. A reporter for the New Orleans *Daily Picayune* inspected the Orleans Parish Prison in 1875 and noted that on "one side are the white prisoners, and on the other side the blacks, so divided for the better preservation of peace and order."[71]

One state institution, the Louisiana Insane Asylum at Jackson, provided no special facilities for black inmates during the period. This was due less to egalitarian ideals than to practical considerations. During the antebellum era, it was widely held that Negroes were incapable of mental illness because of their inferior intelligence and freedom from tensions and vices as a result of their enslavement.[72] On the eve of the Civil War, the institution housed only 1 slave and 10 free Negroes among its 137 patients.[73] Even though black admissions increased sharply during reconstruction,[74] as commitment became an increasingly popular means of dealing with Negroes whose unorthodox behavior did not make them candidates for the penitentiary, the total number of black inmates did not induce asylum officials to set up segregated quarters until after 1877.

On paper the accomplishments of the campaign to destroy the

70. New Orleans *Republican*, Jan. 25, 1874.

71. New Orleans *Daily Picayune*, Mar. 22, 1875.

72. See Elizabeth Wisner, *Public Welfare Administration in Louisiana* (Chicago, 1930), pp. 122–23.

73. *Annual Report of the Board of Administrators of the Insane Asylum at Jackson* (Baton Rouge, 1859), p. 10, cited hereafter as *Report, Insane Asylum*, by year.

74. The report for 1875 claims 38 Negroes out of 167 patients; the 1877 report lists 59 among a total of 194.

color line in places of public accommodation were rather impressive. A constitutional provision outlawed racial segregation, and two state laws and a federal law reinforced the ban. Discrimination was prohibited in the charters of state institutions. Thus, according to the letter of the law, Louisiana Negroes were entitled to ride in white railroad cars and steamboat cabins, eat in white restaurants, sit in white theatre boxes, drink in white saloons, sleep in white hotels, and suffer in white hospital wards.

In reality, however, the movement was a failure. A few assertive blacks demanded and won seats in empty white theatres and doctored drinks in white taverns. One Negro was even awarded one thousand dollars when the latter privilege was denied him. But the overwhelming majority of black Louisianians never saw the inside of a white coach, restaurant, or saloon unless they were employed there as servants. Even in state institutions under the control of Republican-appointed administrators, Negroes were nearly always assigned to separate and generally unequal facilities. Despite a Radical reign of nearly nine years, supported by Republican administrations in Washington and federal military forces in the state, segregation in Louisiana survived the persistent efforts of Negroes and a few whites to kill it.

This failure had several contributing causes. Nearly all whites were opposed to sharing what they considered to be "social" facilities with Negroes. As the Natchitoches *Times* expressed it, "It may be prejudice, or it may be pride, but the feeling of aversion to a perfect social equality with the blacks is inherent in our nature, and may be called an instinct. It exists everywhere, and has existed throughout all time. We cannot stifle it."[75] In the country parishes, where the law had never been wholly impersonal, Republican rule prompted new extremes in vigilante justice. Here, the never-distant white recourse to the rope or the shotgun inevitably made black forays against the color line too hazardous

75. Quoted in the Shreveport *South-Western*, Apr. 15, 1868.

to attempt. Even in New Orleans, where concentrated federal strength and a courageous Negro community made attempts possible, intransigent whites resorted to defiance, then chicanery, to evade the laws.

A second, perhaps more basic, cause for failure in New Orleans was the inability of the Negro leaders to convince the black masses that the struggle was really worth the effort. Most New Orleans Negroes could not afford the white luxuries, and few desired to endure the certain discomfort of white hostility to eat a salted meal or quaff a doctored drink. As the New Orleans *Daily Picayune* pointed out, the civil rights laws were not carried out because of "the colored race having only a slow course of redress through the courts, and rendering themselves liable to be not only summarily ejected from but severely injured in any place of resort which they desire to enter on equal terms with the whites."[76]

The civil rights leaders realized that success hinged upon arousing widespread commitments among common Negroes and did their best to make the color line in public accommodations a symbol for all racial consciousness. The New Orleans *Tribune*, spokesman for the movement in its early phases, denounced segregation "because *our manhood is sacrificed. The broad stamp of inferiority is put upon us.*"[77] This argument failed to attract the great mass of humbler Negroes, in part because the goals seemed worth the effort only to those blacks who could afford the white facilities. On one occasion the *Tribune* reassured whites that a civil rights bill would not force them to associate with lower-class Negroes, arguing that a "poor laborer, coming from his hard work, with his soiled clothes, having gained hardly enough to live, will certainly not pretend to come and pay the price charged by the establishments frequented principally by

76. New Orleans *Daily Picayune*, Mar. 6, 1875.
77. New Orleans *Tribune*, Feb. 7, 1869.

the whites."[78] This observation unwittingly laid bare the central weakness of the movement. A campaign of black aristocrats for essentially elitist goals, the quest for desegregated public accommodations was doomed in large part by the narrow limitations of its very nature.

78. *Ibid.*, Jan. 10, 1869.

FIVE

Country Parish Schools, 1868-77

The "black and tan" constitution
that prohibited segregated places of public accommodation also
decreed that every public school in Louisiana be open to all eligible children, white and black alike. In the country parishes this
proviso presented a more serious challenge to the color line than
did the mandate for mixed accommodations. The schools were
state property, under the control of a centralized state agency,
so desegregation would not have to be initiated by private lawsuits. Unlike the campaign for desegregated steamboats and
saloons, which attracted strong support from only urban, well-to-
do Negroes, the struggle for a single system of integrated public
schools appealed to blacks of every station throughout Louisiana,
for nearly all Negroes regarded a quality education as an essential
rung in the ladder to real freedom.

Thomas W. Conway, elected state superintendent of public
education in April, 1868, sympathized fully with the constitutional mandate for mixed schools. A Baptist minister from New
York, Conway came to New Orleans after the Union conquest
as a chaplain to a regiment of Massachusetts Negro soldiers, and
he soon became active in early black welfare work. Appointed
by General Banks in 1864 to head the army's Bureau of Free Labor, he was selected in 1866 to direct Freedmen's Bureau activities
in Louisiana. An excellent choice on ideological grounds, Conway proved somewhat less than adept at public relations. His

unabashed enthusiasm for racial equality enraged many whites, and Conway returned their antipathy in full measure. In the autumn of 1866 he warned that the "southern rebels, when the power is in their hands, will stop at nothing short of extermination. . . . They are looking anxiously to the extermination of the whole negro race from the country."[1] A few weeks later he was abruptly replaced by the more pliable General J. S. Fullerton as part of an apparent "understanding" between President Andrew Johnson and Provisional Governor J. Madison Wells to emasculate the bureau in the state.[2]

Conway went to work for the Union League and soon became one of the organization's most successful orators. Throughout Louisiana and Mississippi he told black audiences of the many virtues of the Republican party. One of his favorite themes was free, universal, desegregated public education.[3] His partisan zeal and popularity among Negroes attracted the attention of leading Louisiana Republicans, including Henry Clay Warmoth. Despite their differences on segregation, the two became close friends. When Warmoth won the gubernatorial nomination in 1868, he secured Conway's place on the ticket as superintendent of public education. During the campaign Conway's views were vilified by the conservative press. According to the New Orleans *Times*, "If he had been born a woman he would have been the queen of scandal; if a monkey or gorilla, the disgrace of the menagerie; but being only a man, he is simply a slanderer, an apostate, and a carpet-bagger."[4]

Once in office, Conway confirmed the worst fears of his white supremacist critics. Unlike his friend Warmoth, the new super-

1. Quoted in Fleming, *Documentary History of Reconstruction*, I, pp. 362–63.
2. J. Thomas May, "The Politics of Social Welfare: The Decline of the Freedman's Bureau in Louisiana," unpublished paper delivered at the Missouri Valley History Conference in Omaha, Nebr., Mar. 12, 1971, pp. 1–14.
3. New Orleans *Tribune*, June 5, 1867.
4. New Orleans *Times*, Mar. 24, 1868.

intendent placed precious little faith in the "good sense ... and inherent love of justice" of native whites and no confidence that such latent traits would result in the "gradual wearing-away" of their racism. During the summer of 1868, while the governor was grandly promoting his "moderate and discreet" approach to race relations, Conway was quietly preparing a public school bill designed to bring about mandatory school desegregation by requiring compulsory attendance. The bill stipulated that all children between the ages of eight and fourteen were to attend school for at least six months a year. If the parents or guardians, after one warning, refused to enroll their children, a justice of the peace could fine them twenty-five dollars for the first offense and fifty dollars for each subsequent infraction. If the parents ignored three admonitions, the bill required the state board of education to place the children in a school of its choice for at least five months a year, at the expense of the parents if they could afford it.[5]

This plan was altogether unrealistic. It must be remembered that public education was still in its infancy in Louisiana. Apart from New Orleans, which had operated a municipal school system before the war, public schools were virtually nonexistent in antebellum Louisiana.[6] The very idea of free public education financed by taxation was opposed by many Roman Catholics with parochial school systems of their own, by wealthy families who could afford academies or private tutors, and by many poor but proud Louisianians who still equated public education with "pauper schools."[7] Moreover, the sheer physical problem of building a system of public schools throughout the state was monumental. In nearly every community the work had to start from

5. New Orleans *Daily Picayune*, Aug. 11, 1868.

6. A state public school system was established by the constitution of 1845, and some schools were operated in rural Louisiana, but the system broke down before the Civil War. See Shugg, *Origins of Class Struggle*, pp. 69–75.

7. Thomas H. Harris, *The Story of Public Education in Louisiana* (New Orleans, 1924), p. 4; *Report of the Superintendent*, 1871, pp. 119, 132; 1873, p. 223.

scratch. Funds for construction, supplies, and salaries had to come from the taxation of a citizenry impoverished by a military de-defeat and the consequent economic dislocation. Without the resources to educate a fraction of the children of Louisiana, a law requiring the compulsory education of all of them was patently ridiculous.

Moreover, the constitutional ban on "separate schools . . . established exclusively for any race" compounded the difficulties enormously. Without the support of the native whites, such necessities as adequate buildings, literate instructors and administrators, and local financial aid were simply not available in many communities. Abhorred by the whites as "chambers of amalgamation," the public schools in many areas became totally dependent upon the meager economic resources and limited training of local Negroes. Conway's proposal added the possibility of danger to the certainty of inadequacy. Compulsory attendance would force white parents to choose between racial integration and physical resistance. The New Orleans *Daily Picayune* predicted that passage of the bill "will stir up civil war, if nothing else will."[8] But fainter hearts than Conway's prevailed in the legislature, for the measure was quietly buried in committee.

An act setting up the state system of public education was finally passed in 1869, minus the compulsory attendance feature. Section eighty-one prohibited all parishes, municipalities, school officials, and teachers from turning away any child between the ages of six and twenty-one who was entitled to admission by state law and local school board regulations. Violation was classified a misdemeanor, punishable by a fine of not less than one hundred dollars nor more than five hundred dollars and by imprisonment in the parish jail for a period of not less than one month nor longer than six months. To expedite prosecution, the law decreed that "all such causes shall have preference before other criminal cases upon the docket of the court before which it [*sic*] shall be

8. New Orleans *Daily Picayune*, Aug. 11, 1868.

brought." In addition to these rather severe penalties, the law stated that "such persons so offending shall also be liable to an action for damages by the parent or guardian of the child so refused."[9]

Determination to uphold the law and remold the schools marked Conway's first year in office. In his annual report to the legislature for 1869 he declared that "the right of any child to admission into any school of the district in which he resides, and to which he is by law entitled, is one that must be enforced." A "republican State," according to Conway, "can make no distinction between those who are equally citizens, nor can any humiliating conditions be made in the bestowment of benefits to which all have an equal claim." But a year's experience led him to inject a note of caution. "The removal of prejudices, however irrational," he noted, "is rarely the work of a day. . . . In all great changes . . . time is needed for the public mind to adjust itself to the change. . . . At such times a too precipitate attempt to force desirable reforms might delay their secure establishment."[10]

Conway's second thoughts were well founded, for the initial attempts to bring about school desegregation encountered uncompromising white resistance. In Algiers, where a predominantly white electorate had voted in a Democratic school administration, four public schools were in operation in 1869: two for whites and two for blacks. When a Republican executive committee in New Orleans brought this to the attention of the state board of education, Conway wrote to M. M. Lowe, secretary of the Algiers board, demanding an explanation of this breach of the law. In his reply, Lowe told Conway that when the board was formed two black schools run by the American Missionary Association were already in operation in the community. According to Lowe, the schools remained segregated solely out of consideration for Negro parents, who wanted to keep their children in the

9. *Acts of Louisiana,* 1869, no. 121, pp. 175–89.
10. *Report of the Superintendent,* 1869, pp. 12–13.

same schools under the same teachers. Despite angry protests from local Negroes active in Republican politics, the schools in Algiers remained segregated.[11] This incident was altogether typical of many successful local efforts in blocking school desegregation.

White opposition to mixed schooling was virtually universal throughout rural Louisiana. Some white supremacists condemned the very idea of educating Negroes. For example, the Livingston *Herald* complained bitterly in 1870: "It is worse than throwing money away to give it to the education of niggers. . . . To the devil with the present school system."[12] But most whites could tolerate it as long as the races were strictly segregated. The Benton *Bossier Banner* reported that it was "glad to see the education of the blacks growing in favor with our people," but it warned that "Conway's plan of having both races educated together cannot be carried out."[13] Claiming "no ill will to the colored people as a class," the editor of the Clinton *Patriot-Democrat* added, "I say emphatically that the white race is superior to them socially, intellectually, and morally, and any movement or attempt to place them on a footing with us, or us with them, socially must fail."[14]

The stigma of racial integration virtually ruled out any possible cooperation from rural whites. Those who had the education and standing in the community to measurably assist the program usually refused to accept positions as teachers or directors. Sympathetic whites who might have been willing to serve, according to Conway, "have, in many instances, been deterred from accepting the trust by the apprehension of persecution, and

11. Louisiana State Board of Education, *Proceedings and Minutes, 1869–1909* (microfilm copy, Louisiana State University), Dec. 23, 1869, cited hereafter as *Proceedings and Minutes*; Conway to Lowe, Jan. 4, 1870, and Lowe to Conway, Jan. 11, 1870, in Louisiana State Department of Education Correspondence, Orleans Parish, Louisiana State University Archives, cited hereafter as Education Correspondence, by parish.

12. Livingston *Herald*, Feb. 16, 1870.

13. Benton *Bossier Banner*, Apr. 2, 1870.

14. Clinton *Patriot-Democrat*, July 10, 1875.

even social ostracism, on the part of the opponents of the law."[15] When Second District Superintendent Ephraim S. Stoddard was introduced to a prominent citizen in one of the parishes in his division, the man told him, "I wish you success, sir, but I can inform you, beforehand, that you will be the most unpopular man in the parish."[16]

Throughout the country parishes, the desegregation decree was almost always disobeyed or circumvented. Evasion of the law took different forms in different areas, depending upon local conditions. In the Florida parishes of southeastern Louisiana no attempt was made to mix the schools. In early 1869 Dr. R. C. Richardson, district superintendent of education, called upon the editor of the Clinton *East Feliciana Democrat* and informed him "that in arranging the public schools of this district, they will not be mixed, the whites and blacks being entirely separate."[17] Although official reports did not classify students by race, private correspondence from southeastern Louisiana attested to the total, unchallenged racial separation practiced there. Elizabeth C. Booth, in a letter to Conway pleading for back salary, referred to herself as "a teacher in the public school for colored children" in Ponchatoula, and Thomas Garahy, writing for the same reason, identified himself as the former principal of the "white school" in the town. Herman C. Collins, a resident of rural Tangipahoa Parish, wrote Conway in 1871 to protest the absence of a school near his home. According to Collins there were "thirty five children within two miles—half of them are white but the school director here won't have a school because the black and white children would be together."[18]

In the northern parishes of the state the racial character of the

15. *Report of the Superintendent,* 1870, p. 28.
16. *Ibid.,* p. 61.
17. Clinton *East Feliciana Democrat,* Feb. 27, 1869.
18. Booth to Conway, Apr. 14, 1870; Garahy to Conway, May 5, 1870; Collins to Conway, Feb. 1, 1871, all in Education Correspondence, Tangipahoa Parish.

schools often depended upon the political persuasion of the school board. Where white Democrats held power, Negroes were not only kept out of the white schools but were also frequently denied facilities of their own. M. H. Twitchell complained to Conway in 1870 that the Democratic school board in De Soto Parish had given all of the public schools to white children, excluding the Negroes altogether. In a letter to William G. Brown, a Negro who succeeded Conway as state superintendent in 1873, a black Bossier Parish director complained that he was scorned as a "damned nigger teacher" but noted that if he resigned the board would be dominated totally by the Democrats and then "goodbye to colored education in Bossier." James Brewster reported in 1874 that the Democratic board in Bienville Parish had allocated seven of the ten public schools to white children, despite the huge numerical majority of Negroes in the parish.[19]

The white prejudice against school integration was so strong in northern Louisiana that many communities would not tolerate white teachers in the Negro schools. Bowson Holmes of Bossier Parish wrote Conway in 1871 requesting "a lady teacher in the city (colored) who desires to teach a school of females." W. Jasper Blackburn, editor of the Homer *Iliad* and prominent conservative Republican, asked Conway in 1872 "to send us a colored teacher, to teach a colored school." Edwin Sherwood, a northern-born teacher who had lived in the South for many years, complained to Conway that he was unable to secure an appointment in the Bienville schools "because I agree to teach black children. They have the same right to a good teacher as if they were white. I perpose doing and taking the same pains to educate or learn them as if white."[20]

19. Twitchell to Conway, May 25, 1870, in Education Correspondence, De Soto Parish; Bossier Parish school board member to Brown, Dec. 8, 1875, in Education Correspondence, Bossier Parish; Brewster to M. C. Cole, Aug. 27, 1874, in Education Correspondence, Ouachita Parish.

20. Holmes to Conway, May 6, 1871, in Education Correspondence, Bossier Parish; Blackburn to Conway, Feb. 10, 1872, in Education Cor-

In other northern Louisiana districts whites and Negroes apparently quietly agreed to ignore official directives and maintain separate schools. In many of these communities a measure of white support was achieved, and the systems operated with little friction. Samuel J. Powell, a school director in Bayou Sara, reported to divisional superintendent James McCleery in 1870, "I have excited in the minds of our good citizens an interest in this school question—and with an assurance from you to me . . . that there will be no attempt to mix the schools, I have induced some of our best men, in their respective wards, to accept the appointments." W. O. Davis, a school director in Athens, explained to Conway in 1871 that the Claiborne Parish board had set up two schools for whites and one for blacks, "the Freedmen refusing to send their children with the whites." The public schools in Ouachita Parish were originally boycotted by wary white parents, but in 1874 director James Brewster reported record enrollments in the schools in western Ouachita, "both white and colored." Three months later Brewster observed proudly that Morehouse Parish now had twenty-two public schools in operation, explaining that "the colored people have had their full share of the benefits."[21]

Segregation was maintained with similar success in the public schools of rural southern Louisiana, particularly where the great strength of the Roman Catholic church provided a choice between the state system and the parochial schools. Attempting to justify the small number of white students in the St. Martinville public schools in 1873, the secretary of the St. Martin Parish board reported, "This is a Catholic community, and the clergy

---

respondence, Claiborne Parish; Sherwood to Conway, Jan. 28, 1872, in Education Correspondence, Bienville Parish.

21. Powell to McCleery, June 25, 1870, in Education Correspondence, Caddo Parish; Davis to Conway, Feb. 15, 1871, in Education Correspondence, Claiborne Parish; Charles G. Austin, Jr., to Thomas W. Conway, June 11, 1870, and Brewster to M. C. Cole, July 30, Oct. 11, 1874, in Education Correspondence, Ouachita Parish.

of that church are not friendly to free public instruction." The treasurer of the Jefferson Parish school board reported that Catholic clergymen in the parish were leading the opposition against the public schools and "are doing all in their power to establish schools of their own, which are, strictly speaking, anti-Republican, and dangerous to free government." A similar frustration led J. L. Belden, treasurer of the Terrebonne Parish board, to note, "My observation has convinced me that the colored race manifest a far deeper interest in education than the whites."[22]

Coupled with religious misgivings, hostility toward racial equality resulted in white indifference toward the public schools throughout Catholic Louisiana. George W. Combs, board treasurer in St. John the Baptist Parish, reported in 1871 that local whites were maintaining a number of private schools but observed that "out of the five public schools now in operation in this parish, four of them are taught in churches belonging to the colored people." George E. Bovee, secretary of state from 1868 to 1872 and later treasurer of the St. James Parish school board, reported in 1874 that none of the fifteen public schools in the parish was patronized by the whites except "one located in a district where there are few colored children." A report from Jefferson Parish in 1871 indicated that of the five public schools on the left bank of the Mississippi River, "four of them are attended exclusively by colored children, and the fifth by whites."[23]

Public school officials in southern Louisiana made no effort to hide their beliefs that fears of racial integration were responsible for the white hostility to the state schools. Treasurer McKay of Jefferson reported, "The whites will not mix in the schools with the blacks, and any attempt to mix them will prove disastrous to the public school system." In St. James Parish, according to Bovee, "All attempts to establish mixed schools seemed to have

22. *Report of the Superintendent*, 1873, p. 223; 1871, pp. 130, 132.
23. *Ibid.*, 1871, pp. 132, 136; 1874, p. 136.

proved failures, and will continue so until the existing prejudices against color are removed." Voicing a nearly universal complaint among rural school officials, Bovee reported that "the intelligent white people of the parish take little or no interest in the public schools" and advised his superiors that "the work of public education would be much easier, and would advance far more rapidly, without engendering ill-feeling between the races, if the schools were separate."[24]

In those southern Louisiana communities where Bovee's advice was accepted by local Negroes and school officials, a measure of white support was usually achieved. Many white parents enrolled their children, interracial controversies were kept to a minimum, and the public school systems often prospered. By 1871 Iberville Parish was operating thirteen public schools, five for whites and eight for blacks, with a total enrollment of nearly one thousand students. Reporting similar results in Iberia Parish in 1871, the New Iberia *Times* explained, "We have it from a good source that the colored people of our parish do not want mixed schools, and . . . they are not going to apply for admission into the white schools when they have houses prepared for them."[25]

The best contemporary commentary on the problems of public education in rural southern Louisiana is found in the diary, correspondence, and official reports of Ephraim S. Stoddard, superintendent of the second division throughout the reconstruction. Born in Vermont in 1837, Stoddard migrated to Illinois, served during the war as a sergeant in the Seventy-seventh Illinois Volunteers, was captured in the vicinity of Mansfield, Louisiana, and spent the last thirteen months of the conflict in a Confederate prison camp. After Appomattox he remained in Louisiana, labored for two years as a school administrator for the Freedmen's Bureau, worked briefly as secretary of the state board of education, and

24. *Ibid.*, 1871, p. 132; 1874, p. 136.
25. Quoted in *ibid.*, 1871, p. 205.

served as a divisional superintendent in the sugar parishes from 1869 to 1877.[26]

Even more than his friend and superior Conway, Stoddard exemplified the visionary spirit of northern egalitarianism. In a letter to his brother, he prophesied that the *"Typical American"* was being created by "the blending and fusing of every nation and every race created by God," proclaiming, *"A unified race—* what a thought! The idea excites the power of my mind to follow. When its completion has been wrought—then is the millenium."[27] According to Stoddard, the Negro would be "swallowed up, not by extermination but by absorption." He dismissed white revulsion over racial amalgamation by pointing out, "You have saved me the trouble, my Southern friend, of advocating that doctrine . . . for there is not a family to the manor born south of 'Mason and Dixon's line' whose blood does not course freely in the veins of Africa."[28]

Stoddard's unfettered optimism was buffeted considerably in the sugar parishes. In his annual report to Conway for 1871, he offered a rather harsh but nevertheless realistic appraisal of the difficulties confronting public school desegregation. Describing the upper-class whites as "never friendly to public education at all," he pointed out that they generally chose to send their children to "private institutions, sometimes at home, but more commonly abroad." He portrayed the poorer whites as victims of a dilemma, unable to afford private schooling but "reared as they have been in superstition and ignorance . . . they will be the last to patronize a school that admits a colored child to a seat therein. . . . Uneducated themselves, their appreciation of learning is not equal to their prejudice deeply rooted in superstitious ignorance."[29] Stoddard's experiences frequently confirmed these ob-

26. Ephraim S. Stoddard Papers, Tulane University Archives.
27. Ephraim S. Stoddard to H. R. Stoddard, Jan. 12, 1875, Ephraim S. Stoddard Papers, Tulane University Archives.
28. *Ibid.*, Jan. 12, 18, 1875.
29. Quoted in *Report of the Superintendent*, 1871, pp. 119–20.

servations. In a diary entry in 1875, he recorded that a teacher in Roseland had reported to him that "white people will not permit her to teach a mixed school and there are not children enough for two schools."[30]

In a few extremely rare instances, desegregated schools were operated in the back settlements of the sugar parishes. J. W. Burke informed Conway in July, 1870, that he was teaching a small school with eleven white children and fifteen Negroes at Bayou Mangoin in the remote wilderness of the Atchafalaya marshes. According to Burke's enthusiastic report, "Most of them did not know their alphabets now they can spell well, as well as read."[31] Another racially integrated public school was maintained with evident success in rural Lafourche Parish. It was taught by Colonel A. Laforest, described by Stoddard as "an old planter of the parish, and . . . a highly educated gentleman," on his own plantation. Stoddard reported in 1875 that the school was "about equally attended by white and colored children" and reiterated Laforest's assurance that "there was not the least difficulty on that account."[32] The success of this arrangement was probably less attributable to the new doctrines of racial equality than to the old patterns of plantation life. Laforest apparently taught the children of his former slaves and those of a few white neighbors, secure from criticism by his social position and by the tacit understanding that plantation children of both races had always associated with each other without confusing caste priorities.

There may have been other public schools in rural southern Louisiana in which white and black children studied together, but references are vague. S. C. Mollere, secretary of the Assumption Parish school board, reported in 1871 that in certain un-

30. Ephraim S. Stoddard Diary, May 26, 1875, Tulane University Archives.

31. Burke to Conway, July 28, 1870, in Education Correspondence, Iberville Parish.

32. *Report of the Superintendent,* 1875, p. 142.

named communities "children of both colors have attended schools in common, and in such schools the improvement of the pupils was astonishing . . . accounted for, I suppose, by the constant emulation between the two races."[33] Third Division Superintendent R. K. Diossy reported in 1871 that virtually all of the public schools in the southwestern parishes were segregated "by the choice of both children and parents of all classes," but alluded vaguely to schools in isolated settlements attended by white and black children together.[34] These mixed schools most likely resulted from longstanding familiarity between local whites and Negroes, not from any discernible commitment to the Republican doctrine of racial equality. Whatever the explanation, integrated schools remained oddities throughout the country parishes.

Displeasure over public school policies led many white parents to support secular and parochial private schools in the country parishes. In many Catholic communities systems of parochial schools begun before the Civil War were greatly expanded during the reconstruction. Although whites and blacks still worshipped together at this time in most Catholic churches, schools operated by the denomination were strictly segregated. Such orders as the Sisters of St. Joseph, Sisters of the Holy Family, and Sisters of the Sacred Heart began Negro schools in Baton Rouge, Opelousas, and Grand Coteau during the 1870s, but the vast majority of Catholic schools were supported for and by white parents alarmed over the twin dangers of secularism and egalitarianism in the public schools.[35]

Most country parish private schools, however, were nondenominational institutions established by individual entrepreneurs and educators. Remarkably diverse, these private schools

33. *Ibid.*, 1871, p. 199.
34. *Ibid.*, p. 189.
35. Sister Mary David Young, "A History of the Development of Catholic Education for the Negro in Louisiana" (M.A. thesis, Louisiana State University, 1944), pp. 29, 37, 59–62, 67–68.

varied in quality from truly excellent academies to pathetic operations run by functional illiterates. Physical plants ranged from elegant mansions to abandoned sheds. In many communities the great majority of white schoolchildren attended such institutions. Negroes totally monopolized the Alexandria public schools until 1873, and as late as December, 1875, the Alexandria *Louisiana Democrat* could complain that the only white public school in town was held in an "old fly-specked shanty."[36] Official reports for 1875 indicated that the twenty-two public schools in Rapides Parish were nearly all for Negroes and that nine private schools were educating 905 white students.[37] This situation was by no means unique. In 1874 in the second division, Stoddard estimated that 2,301 white children were enrolled in private schools and only 805 in the public system.[38] Often poorly financed and frequently short-lived, these independent private schools nevertheless gave the rudiments of an education to a large number of white boys and girls whose parents feared the racial policies of the public schools.

One attempt was made during the reconstruction to establish a statewide system of white schools. In February, 1867, philanthropist George Peabody, a New England financier and merchant, endowed a fund to be used to help develop education in the South.[39] A year later the Peabody trustees appointed former State Superintendent Robert Mills Lusher to administer the fund's aid to schools in Louisiana. An outspoken racist who viewed education as a means to "vindicate the honor and supremacy of the Caucasian race," Lusher used the Peabody grants and local con-

36. Alexandria *Louisiana Democrat*, Dec. 15, 1875; William Edward Highsmith, "Social and Economic Conditions in Rapides Parish during Reconstruction" (M.A. thesis, Louisiana State University, 1947), p. 122; William David McKay, "History of Education in Rapides Parish, 1805–1915" (M.A. thesis, Louisiana State University, 1936), p. 45.
37. *Report of the Superintendent*, 1875, pp. 234, 292.
38. *Ibid.*, 1874, p. 270.
39. R. Freeman Butts and Lawrence A. Kremin, *A History of Education in American Culture* (New York, 1953), pp. 411–12.

tributions in an attempt to build an exclusively white school system similar to the one he had established as state superintendent from 1865 to 1868. In August, 1869, the Peabody trustees allocated $11,000 for Louisiana. Lusher used it to supplement $35,000 raised in the state to support white schools in Arcadia, Natchitoches, Bastrop, Homer, Shreveport, Pleasant Hill, Plaquemine, Amite City, Alexandria, Donaldsonville, Franklin, Tangipahoa, Bayou Sara, Clinton, Baton Rouge, Greensburg, Eureka, Franklinton, Algiers, and Gretna.[40]

At its meeting of May 1, 1869, the state board of education had already declared itself the "proper medium for the care and disbursement" of Peabody funds in Louisiana, but the trustees ignored the contention. In October, 1870, Superintendent Conway wrote Peabody General Agent Barnas Sears an attack on Lusher for building a system "antagonistic to that of the State," fomenting a rebellion against the public schools, and placing the Peabody trustees "in the false position of establishing a caste system of education . . . at variance with the declarations put forth by them." Conway suggested that all future Peabody allocations be distributed through his agency to bring about greater efficiency, economy, and democracy. Sears replied that he would like to cooperate with the public school authorities, but that he had been informed that white boycotts over desegregation had created a public school system monopolized by Negroes, thus depriving the poorer white children of Louisiana of the chance to obtain an education. Denying that he or the trustees were in any way passing judgment on the idea of racial integration, Sears justified Lusher's policies on the grounds that "we are helping the white children in Louisiana, as being the more destitute, from the fact of their unwillingness to attend mixed schools."[41]

40. Myrtle H. Rey, "Robert Mills Lusher, Louisiana Educator" (M.A. thesis, Tulane University, 1933), p. 39.

41. *Proceedings and Minutes*, May 1, 1869; Conway to Sears, Oct. 28, 1870, and Sears to Conway, Nov. 8, 1870, both reprinted in *Report of the Superintendent*, 1870, pp. 40–42.

Peabody grants, under Lusher's supervision, continued to finance white private schools and anger Radicals throughout the reconstruction period. In September, 1873, the New Orleans *Republican* complained that Sears was being misled by "a pensioner on the bounty of his trust" to believe "that the destitute children of Louisiana are confined to a class of children known as whites."[42] Lusher's refusal to report enrollment figures and other statistics to State Superintendent William G. Brown on the grounds that Brown was elected by "fraud and actual usurpation" prompted the public school officials to renew demands for Lusher's ouster.[43] But Sears and the Peabody trustees, actively assisting Negro education in southern states where segregation was official policy, retained Lusher as their director in Louisiana and kept limiting grants to white schools in the state throughout the period.

In 1871 the fund allocated $13,800 to supplement $41,445 raised locally to assist six schools in New Orleans and individual schools in Amite City, Arcadia, Bastrop, Baton Rouge, Bayou Sara, Clinton, Columbia, Fairview, Franklinton, Gretna, Harrisonburg, Homer, Livonia, Minden, Monroe, Natchitoches, Plaquemine, Pleasant Hill, Shreveport, Thibodaux, Terre aux Boeufs, and Winnfield. This marked the zenith of Peabody assistance to Louisiana education. In 1872 it disbursed only $7,550 to be used with $36,229 in local contributions to aid schools in Amite City, Arcadia, Columbia, Bayou Sara, Gretna, Clinton, Homer, Montgomery, Pickneyville, Thibodaux, Trenton, and Terre aux Boeufs. By 1873 the Peabody allotments were decreased to $5,940 for sixteen schools, and the 1874 allocation amounted to only $3,250 for schools in Amite City, Minden, New Orleans, Jackson, and Montgomery.[44] Since Peabody funds were given in ratio to local contributions, the declining grants reflected an

42. New Orleans *Republican*, Sept. 28, 1873.
43. *Report of the Superintendent*, 1873, pp. 31–32.
44. Rey, "Robert Mills Lusher," pp. 41–45, 50.

obvious flagging of local white support as the spectre of integration failed to materialize in the country parish public schools.

The struggle over segregation involved one country parish institution of higher learning, the Louisiana State Seminary, located four miles from Alexandria until 1869, when a fire forced it to move to Baton Rouge. The racial ideology prevalent at the seminary was summed up by Trustee G. Mason Graham, a former Confederate general, when he confided to a professorial candidate, "frankly, we are a white man's party, and negrophilists, or those in sympathy with them, can find no favor in our eyes."[45] Its quasi-public status, Confederate heritage, and unreconstructed demeanor made the seminary an inviting target for Republican integrationists. An article requiring the school to accept all students "without distinction of race, color, or previous condition" was dropped from the final version of the constitution of 1868, but the issue was not forgotten by such egalitarians as State Superintendent Conway and many powerful black Radicals.

Governor Warmoth, whose distaste for compulsory desegregation was by no means means limited to public accommodations legislation, was instrumental in shielding the school from a confrontation over its admission policies during his term in office. In July, 1868, Seminary President David French Boyd informed former President William Tecumseh Sherman of widespread fears that Warmoth would seize control of the school, but noted, "I do not think so. I had several talks with his Excellency while in N.O., and believe that he will not interfere with us, unless *party pressure* becomes much greater."[46] His prediction proved correct. Warmoth supported the conservative board of supervisors of the seminary throughout his term and, without exception, followed Boyd's recommendations in naming new trustees

45. Graham to Fred V. Hopkins, Aug. 4, 1868, in the Walter L. Fleming Collection, G. Mason Graham Papers, Louisiana State University Archives.
46. Boyd to Sherman, July 27, 1868, in the David F. Boyd Letter Book I, 1865–1868, Louisiana State University Archives.

to that board. The student body remained lily-white, yet state funds were appropriated annually. When the seminary was destroyed by fire in 1869, Warmoth personally found temporary quarters for the school in a building belonging to the state deaf and dumb asylum in Baton Rouge.[47]

The crux of the controversy between the integrationists and the school was the "beneficiary" system, a program whereby the police jury of each parish selected two young men to attend the seminary at public expense. General Graham and others feared that Radical police juries would nominate black beneficiaries, thus forcing the school to desegregate or face a virtually certain curtailment of state appropriations.[48] A plan engineered by Superintendent Conway to coerce the seminary to integrate its beneficiary program was thwarted by a compromise, worked out by Warmoth, Boyd, and State Senator J. C. Egan, which extended the beneficiary system to Straight University, a black college in New Orleans.[49]

Despite Warmoth's protection, the seminary, which was renamed Louisiana State University in 1870, remained a choice target for Republican egalitarians. Conway, in particular, continued to entertain hopes of bringing the college under his personal control. Boyd's failure to provide enrollment statistics for 1870 prompted Conway to suggest in his report for that year "the propriety to bringing the University into such a relation to the State Board of Education as will insure possession of the information."[50] In response to a Boyd proposal for free tuition financed by state appropriations, Conway suggested in his 1871 report that "the ends sought by Colonel Boyd would be attained

47. Walter L. Fleming, *Louisiana State University, 1860–1896* (Baton Rouge, 1936), pp. 153–59.

48. Boyd to Warmoth, Dec, 15, 1868, in the Walter L. Fleming Collection, Louisiana State University Official Papers, Louisiana State University Archives.

49. Fleming, *Louisiana State University*, pp. 153–59.

50. *Report of the Superintendent*, 1870, p. 43.

more satisfactorily by an ordinance making the State University a part of the State system of public schools." Noting that he considered free tuition a fine idea, he added pointedly that he looked forward to working with Boyd "on the ground of making it absolutely within the reach of the young men of Louisiana, irrespective of race or color."[51]

Hostility between the university board and the Radicals often flared up over trivial incidents. When some of the students removed an annoying bell from the deaf and dumb asylum, the New Orleans *Republican* exaggerated the prank into a scandal and demanded an official investigation, prompting Boyd to call the *Republican* editor a "miserable cur."[52] Another incident nearly developed into a more serious controversy. Commandant of Cadets Edward Cunningham, egged on by some of his students, refused to shake hands with two black legislators touring the campus. The outraged representatives threatened retaliatory measures. Cunningham offered his resignation to protect the school, but Boyd rejected it, secured written apologies from the guilty cadets, and advised trustee W. L. Sanford, "I think it best to let it die, as it seems to be doing."[53] Boyd's prognosis seemed correct at the time, for the offended legislators could not garner enough support from their colleagues to force Warmoth to take a stand on the matter, and the uproar gradually subsided.

Eventually, however, the university was forced to pay an enormous price for its arrogant elitism and white supremacist admissions policies. Relations between the school and the state government deteriorated rapidly after Warmoth's fall from power. Unlike his predecessor, William Pitt Kellogg had little sympathy for racial segregation and even less for a college run by men diametrically opposed to his political persuasion. As soon

51. *Ibid.*, 1871, pp. 26–29.
52. Boyd to W. L. Sanford, Dec. 23, 1871, in the David F. Boyd Letters, Louisiana State University Archives.
53. Boyd to Sanford, Mar. 7, 1871, in *ibid.*; Fleming, *Louisiana State University*, p. 195.

as the 1873 legislative session began, integrationists revived their campaign to force the university to admit black cadets. When Boyd and the trustees refused to do this, the legislature abruptly withdrew all financial support, including funds for the beneficiary cadets.[54]

This gambit placed university officials in a decidedly precarious position. As Boyd complained to Sanford, "Now the legislature won't support us, because we have no negroes here; and the whites are afraid to send us their sons, because the negro may come here."[55] Forced to make the final choice between integration and poverty, Boyd decided to try to keep the school alive without state appropriations "till right, & reason, & enlightenment again have their due might in our Legislature."[56] On March 8, 1873, he discharged the beneficiary cadets, praising them as "our brightest and best boys" and advising them to think of their dismissal "in the light of an indefinite furlough."[57] The session of 1873/74 closed with only 24 cadets, compared with 131 four years earlier. The 1874/75 term began with 10 students and ended with only 4. The university somehow endured for two more years with a handful of cadets; a faculty of Boyd, his brother Thomas, and a cadet-tutor; and seemingly limitless credit from local merchants, until the Democrats regained control of the state government in 1877 and restored financial aid to the school.[58]

In a sense the conflict between the Kellogg administration and the university symbolized the larger struggle between the white citizens of the country parishes and the Republicans over the

54. Fleming, *Louisiana State University*, p. 200.
55. Boyd to Sanford, Apr. 11, 1874, in the David F. Boyd Letters.
56. David F. Boyd Diary, 1874–1875, I, July 23, 1874, Louisiana State University Archives.
57. General Order No. 2, Mar. 8, 1873, in the Walter L. Fleming Collection, Louisiana State University Official Papers.
58. Boyd to Sanford, July 27, Oct. 26, 1874, in the David F. Boyd Letters; "Commencement Remarks of D. F. Boyd, Superintendent, to the Cadets of Louisiana State University, June 30, 1875," typescript, Walter L. Fleming Collection, Louisiana State University Official Papers.

racial composition of the public schools. In October, 1867, nearly six months before the voters made school integration a part of Louisiana law, the New Orleans *Tribune* predicted that economic inevitabilities would guarantee the success of the arrangement. Arguing that a "father of four or five children will not pay three dollars a month, for each of them, for private schools, when he can get them educated freely in the public schools—be it even along side colored children," the *Tribune* observed, "Prejudices are not allowed to affect the pocket as they affect the brain."[59] Ten years of subsequent controversy proved that the *Tribune* was wrong and that rural white Louisianians valued their racial supremacy far more than economic self-interest, political tranquility, or even education itself.

Throughout the country parishes, public school desegregation failed almost universally. In rare instances white and black children studied in the same classrooms in remote back settlements in rural southern Louisiana, but these mixed schools were examples of the survival of plantation hegemony, not manifestations of a new spirit of racial brotherhood. In nearly every community where whites and Negroes did not reach tacit agreements to maintain separate schools, public education was monopolized by one race or the other. In the parishes where public schools were segregated by common consent, they were often attended and supported by whites and blacks alike. On the whole, the cause of public education made substantial advances in rural Louisiana during the reconstruction, but this progress came only after segregation, the sine qua non of country parish race relations, had been firmly established.

59. New Orleans *Tribune*, Oct. 29, 1867.

New Orleans Schools, 1868-77

Unlike the drives to desegregate places of public accommodation and the rural public schools, which produced paper victories but few tangible accomplishments, the campaign to end segregation in the New Orleans public schools developed into a truly remarkable experiment in interracial coexistence. For a period of nearly seven years, at a time when school integration was virtually nonexistent in other southern communities and quite uncommon north of the Ohio, sizeable numbers of white and black children attended the same public schools in New Orleans. This unusual achievement was the high-water mark of the struggle to bring about a new social order in post–Civil War Louisiana.

The racial composition of the city schools had been a central issue in the segregation controversy since September, 1862, when a *café au lait* free Negro girl briefly integrated the student body of the Barracks School until her ancestry was discovered.[1] By the summer of 1867 school desegregation had attained a status second only to the franchise as a source of contention between whites and blacks. Frightened public school officials tried to head off a confrontation by setting up a parallel system of Negro schools, but the black voters responded by selecting delegates to the constitutional convention who forced adoption of Article 135, which forbade "separate schools or institutions of learning established

1. Beasley, "History of Education in Louisiana," pp. 37–38.

exclusively for any race by the State of Louisiana." The "solemn referendum" of April 17 and 18, 1868, failed to settle the question. The statewide majority of black voters made mixed schools the law of Louisiana by ratifying the constitution and electing a Radical Republican administration to enforce it. But in New Orleans, where whites outnumbered Negroes nearly three to one, Democratic mayoralty candidate John Conway led his party to a landslide sweep of all municipal offices, assuring the city of an administration pledged to preserving racial segregation in the public schools.[2]

New Orleans Negroes wasted no time in testing their newly acquired legal rights. In late April, only a few days after ratification, a number of light-skinned Negro girls were admitted to the Bayou Road School. By May 7 the matter had come to the attention of City Superintendent William O. Rogers, who wrote Mrs. S. Bigot, principal of the school, to find out "if there are any children known, or generally reported, to be colored—who are now attending your school."[3] Mrs. Bigot replied that twenty-eight girls of mixed ancestry were enrolled at Bayou Road. One was the daughter of Alderman C. S. Sauvinet, the prominent civil rights activist who later initiated and won the landmark lawsuit against a white tavern owner who had refused to serve him a drink. Nearly all of the girls came from the *gens de couleur*. Mrs. Bigot informed Rogers that she had been deceived by the girls' appearances, but that some of her white students had later exposed the twenty-eight as Negroes, an explanation that prompted one angry school board member to demand her immediate dismissal for "having betrayed the trust reposed in her by the Board of Directors."[4]

2. New Orleans *Daily Picayune*, Apr. 21, 1868.
3. Rogers to Bigot, May 7, 1868, reprinted in the Orleans Parish School Board Minutes, May 21, 1868 (Orleans Parish School Board records office, 703 Carondelet Street, New Orleans).
4. Orleans Parish School Board Minutes, May 21, 1868; Bigot to Rogers, May 21, 1868, reprinted in *ibid*.

School officials acted quickly to prevent any further violations of this nature. In its meeting on May 27, 1868, the board of school directors transferred the twenty-eight girls from Bayou Road into black schools, adopted a resolution decreeing "that all children of color, who may be found in any of the white schools of this City, shall immediately be furnished with a written transfer to the school to which they properly belong," and selected a committee to investigate the Bayou Road incident during the summer recess.[5] On September 2, 1868, the board issued orders that the principals of the white schools be "hereby instructed not to receive any children of color. . . & that the Principals inform said colored applicants that they will be admitted into the schools established by the city for the education of colored children." At the same meeting the investigative committee reported that the segregated school system "is giving satisfaction to all our citizens without regard to 'race, color or previous condition'—except the carpetbaggers."[6]

As far as New Orleans Negroes were concerned, this smug assessment was hopelessly wide of the mark. The briefly resurrected *Tribune* decried almost daily the "odious and unjust restrictions on our liberty."[7] Other blacks exhibited their displeasure more pointedly. On September 25, 1868, a Negro named Edouard Faures was shot to death by a white man in the Vegetable Market, and simmering frustrations in the black community boiled into street rioting. A group of armed Negroes marched to the white Fillmore School, in the Third District, and sent a number of boys into the school to demand admission. When the white students physically repelled the outnumbered black youths, the Negroes outside opened fire on the school.[8] Officials quickly closed the school and averted possible carnage, but the black

5. *Ibid.*, May 27, 1868.
6. *Ibid.*, Sept. 2, 1868.
7. New Orleans *Tribune*, Feb. 4, 1869.
8. New Orleans *Bee*, Sept. 26, 1868.

fusillades offered eloquent evidence that the segregated system of public schools was not "giving satisfaction to all ... without regard to 'race, color or previous condition.' "

The main bulwark against racial change remained the Democratic board of school directors. In September, 1869, the state board of education adopted a regulation that the president of each local school board "shall be required to furnish each youth ... with a printed certificate designating the proper school at which the holder is entitled to attend, and no pupil shall be entitled to admission to any other school."[9] This proposal was designed by State Superintendent Conway to accelerate the process of desegregation by preventing whites from transferring out of mixed schools, but it was perverted by the New Orleans school board into a means of perpetuating segregation in its schools. Warner Van Norden, president of the city board, simply used the issuance of admission permits to assign white children to white schools and black children to black schools, thus eliminating any chance that individual schools could be desegregated through a slipshod screening of transfer students. Using Conway's regulation to its own advantage, the board of school directors managed to thwart all attempts to integrate the city schools throughout the 1869/70 school year.[10]

Outmaneuvered and outraged, Conway decided that he would have to destroy the power of the Democratic board in order to desegregate the New Orleans public schools. During the summer recess of 1870 he began to organize a rival network of "ward" school boards, personally packing them with Negroes and white Radical partisans sympathetic to the idea of mixed schools. A few days before the scheduled opening of the fall term, Conway moved to divert all state funds from the Democratic board to his own ward boards, prompting the desperate conservatives to

9. *Proceedings and Minutes,* Sept. 14, 1869.
10. New Orleans *Daily Picayune,* Jan. 12, 1871.

seek an injunction against the action. On November 21, 1870, Judge Henry C. Dibble,[11] a northern-born Radical appointed to the bench by Governor Warmoth, ruled in Eighth District Court that Conway's ward boards were legally entitled to distribute all state funds allocated to the city public schools.[12] This verdict forced the Democratic board to disband in protest, removing the final administrative barrier against public school desegregation in New Orleans.

Under the sovereignty of the Republican ward boards, the color line began to collapse quickly. During the first week of classes after the Christmas recess, the three adopted daughters of Lieutenant Governor Oscar J. Dunn were admitted into the Madison Girls' School. Eleven black youths were permitted to enroll in formerly white boys' schools, six in the Bienville Boys' School and five in the St. Philip Boys' School. A *Daily Picayune* investigation of the school situation disclosed on January 12, 1871, that "the mixing of the public schools has silently and gradually been going on ever since the Ward Boards assumed control."[13]

White New Orleanians had been given nearly three years to prepare themselves for the possibility of school desegregation, but when it finally came to pass their shock was obvious. One white supremacist wrote, "Great God, I wonder that the spirits of our dead do not rise up to jeer and scoff us when such degradation of soul is witnessed. Me thinks I see Lee, Jackson, and a host of their compeers standing upon the eternal shore with faces veiled in shame and sad tears rising at the sight of their people so fallen."[14] When Negroes were admitted to the Bienville Boys' School, an estimated 175 white students, nearly half of

11. Dibble was the same judge who, five months later, ruled that C. S. Sauvinet was entitled to one thousand dollars from J. A. Walker under the Louisiana Civil Rights Act of 1869.

12. New Orleans *Daily Picayune*, Nov. 22, 1870.

13. *Ibid.*, Jan. 12, 1871.

14. Quoted in the New Orleans *Republican*, Feb. 5, 1871.

the total enrollment, were withdrawn by their parents. Similar reactions decimated the ranks of other city schools, including the Claiborne Boys' School and the Pontchartrain School in Milneburg.[15]

A massive white reaction against the desegregation of the public schools was largely responsible for the greatest private school boom in the history of the city. In August, 1867, New Orleanian Willie T. Nicholls informed an Ascension Parish relative that the family was seeking a larger home to use as a private school, explaining that "the public schools are to have negroes, so that white children will have to go to paying schools."[16] Nicholls' timing may have been rather premature, but his prediction proved accurate once the desegregation actually began. The chaos of war and occupation had all but destroyed private education in New Orleans. In 1868 only ten private schools were listed in the city directory, and eight of those were Roman Catholic parochial schools.[17] But the prohibition of segregated public schools in the constitution of 1868 and subsequent attempts to implement that edict led to a phenomenal multiplication of private schools of every variety.

Most numerous were the nondenominational schools run individually for financial profit, usually by educated women or even whole families in dire economic straits. Although a few of these institutions occupied spacious rented facilities, the great majority of them were located in private homes beneath the living quarters of the proprietors. In 1868 there were only two such schools operating in the city, but by 1869 the number jumped

15. New Orleans *Daily Picayune*, June 23, 1871; *Report of the Superintendent*, 1871, pp. 374–75, 389.

16. Nicholls to Thomas B. Pugh, Aug. 11, 1867, in the W. W. Pugh and Family Papers, Louisiana State University Archives.

17. Mary DiMartini, "Education in New Orleans during Reconstruction" (M.A. thesis, Tulane University, 1935), pp. 159–81, consists of appendices of the names and years in operation of all Catholic, Protestant, and nondenominational private schools listed in the New Orleans city directories from 1866 to 1877.

to nineteen. By 1870, when the Republican wards boards took control of the public schools, the total skyrocketed to fifty-one. Between 1871 and 1877 the number of these nondenominational private schools fluctuated between forty-seven and sixty-three.[18] A few achieved financial success and enjoyed relative permanence, but the great majority survived for only a year or two, offering their students white classmates and very little else.

The Roman Catholic parochial schools operated by the Archdiocese of New Orleans and the various teaching orders offered white Catholic children an alternative to the desegregated public schools and the jerry-built nondenominational institutions. Before the Civil War the Catholic church had maintained a number of institutions, mostly exclusive academies and charity schools. The growth of the public school system after the war spurred Catholic officials to expand their educational system in an effort to combat what they regarded as creeping secularism. During the reconstruction years the church began to build a parish-by-parish school system that soon rivaled the public system in both quantity and quality. Completely segregated, the Catholic system profited immensely from the dislocation of pupils caused by the desegregation of the public schools. The number of Catholic schools increased from two in 1866 and 1867 to eight in 1868 and eleven in 1869. In 1870, when the ward boards captured control of the public schools, the number of Catholic institutions doubled to twenty-two. They increased to thirty-four in 1871, forty in 1872, forty-five in 1873, and forty-nine in 1874 and 1875.[19] Although this proliferation coincided with postwar economic recovery and rising fears of secularism, Catholic school expansion clearly received its greatest impetus from the white exodus from the public schools.

The school integration crisis brought into being a third type of private institution, the Protestant parochial school. Fewer in

18. *Ibid.*, pp. 159–71.
19. *Ibid.*, pp. 172–78.

number than either the nondenominational or Catholic schools, these Protestant facilities followed similar growth patterns. There were none before 1870, but in that year the Evangelical Lutheran Congregation School, the Evangelical Lutheran School, and the German Evangelical Protestant School were also begun. By 1871 ten such schools were being run by the Lutherans, Methodists, Episcopalians, and Presbyterians. Twelve Protestant institutions were in operation in 1872, a number that remained constant until 1877. German-Americans, probably less concerned with white supremacy than with the preservation of their Old World heritage, added a Lutheran school, two Evangelical schools, and two German Presbyterian schools to the three they had founded in 1870. The Methodists limited their activity to the short-lived Southern Methodist High School. The Episcopalians organized the Church Education Society in 1870 to supervise their parochial school endeavors. During the 1870s schools were founded and supported by four Episcopal congregations: Annunciation, Calvary, Christ, and Trinity.[20]

The most thoroughgoing of all Protestant programs in New Orleans was that of the Presbyterian church. Dominated by the powerful Benjamin M. Palmer of First Church, an outspoken advocate of slavery, secession, and white supremacy, the Presbyterians reacted strongly against public school desegregation. Convinced that the "forcible mingling of races in the school room and upon the playground would . . . end in strife, hostility, and the ultimate destruction of the schools,"[21] the Presbyterians organized a school board during the summer of 1870 and appointed William O. Rogers, the former city public school superintendent, to coordinate a parochial school system. Six grammar schools, a boys' academy, and the Sylvester Larned Institute for Girls opened in September, 1870. Supported by tuition fees and church contributions, the Presbyterian school system remained in

20. *Ibid.*, pp. 179–81; Carter and Carter, *So Great a Good*, pp. 162–63.
21. New Orleans *Southwestern Presbyterian*, May 26, 1870.

operation until school desegregation ended in 1877. The Sylvester Larned Institute, directed by Rogers and affiliated with Palmer's First Church, was widely regarded as an excellent girls' academy until it closed its doors in 1881, bringing to an end the Presbyterian experiment in parochial education.[22]

The enormous proliferation of nondenominational, Roman Catholic, and Protestant private schools after 1868 was a direct white reaction to the desegregation of the city's public schools. The number of private institutions in New Orleans mushroomed from ten in 1868 to ninety-one in 1871, the first year that Negroes were admitted into the white public schools. From 1872 to 1877 more than one hundred private schools of all types were in operation in the city. No reliable statistics on the overall enrollment in these schools are available,[23] but William O. Rogers's official report for 1877 estimated that 16,000 white children were then attending private schools, as opposed to only 15,169 whites in the city's public schools.[24] Evidence that the parents of more than half of the white students chose to pay tuition to keep their children in segregated schools bears witness to the deep revulsion they felt toward school integration.

White boycotting of the mixed public schools, however, was by no means a universal phenomenon. In some desegregated schools black students were introduced with a minimum of controversy. At other schools initially decimated by mass white withdrawals, conditions rapidly returned to normal. Officials at the Pontchartrain School in Milneburg reported in December, 1871, that "children, who were withdrawn, from a dissatisfac-

22. *Ibid.*, Aug. 18, Sept. 15, Oct. 6, 1870; July 6, 1871; Julia McGowan, "The Presbyterian Churches in New Orleans during Reconstruction" (M.A. thesis, Tulane University, 1939), pp. 3–11.

23. As Louis R. Harlan pointed out in "Desegregation in New Orleans Schools during Reconstruction," *American Historical Review*, LXVII (Apr., 1962), p. 669, the total white private school enrollment figures for 1869 cited by contemporaries ranged from State Superintendent Conway's estimate of 1,200 to City Superintendent Rogers's estimate of 15,000.

24. *Report of the Superintendent*, 1877, pp. 12, 315.

tion with the enforcement of constitutional requirements, have returned, and the principal reports prospects favorable for the future." E. Warren Smith, principal of the Bienville School, half emptied by a white exodus in January, 1871, reported less than a year later, "Two-thirds of the pupils are white and one-third colored. It is but seldom that the usual peace and good order of the school are disturbed by any exhibitions of prejudice on account of race or color." [25]

Although the great majority of students remained in private schools or public schools that were not yet desegregated, the progress made toward public school integration during 1871 was undeniably impressive. William Rollinson, secretary of the new Republican school board in New Orleans, stated that desegregation had been put into practice during the year in a number of city schools without "any of the unfavorable results so freely predicted in advance of the honest trial of an impartial system of education." The year's advances prompted Superintendent Conway to exult, "Justice has triumphed, and to-day our schools, though open to all, regardless to color, are in a more flourishing condition than before we took control of them." [26]

After the initial shock of adjustment, public school desegregation proceeded quite smoothly from the spring of 1871 through the summer of 1874. According to Louis R. Harlan's excellent study of the experiment, between five hundred and one thousand black children and several thousand white pupils were enrolled in no fewer than nineteen mixed New Orleans public schools in the spring of 1874. [27] In the Second and Third Districts below

25. New Orleans *Daily Picayune*, June 23, 1871; *Report of the Superintendent*, 1871, pp. 375, 389.

26. *Report of the Superintendent*, 1871, pp. 308, 360.

27. Harlan, "Desegregation in New Orleans Schools," p. 666, designated Barracks, Bayou Bridge, Beauregard, Bienville, Central Boys' High, Claiborne, Fillmore, Fisk, Franklin, Keller, Lower Girls' High, Madison, Paulding, Pontchartrain, Rampart, Robertson, St. Anne, St. Philip, Spain, and Webster as desegregated schools and Cut-off Road, Dunn, Gentilly, and McDonoughville as possibly mixed. Central Boys' High and Paulding

Canal Street, where the white population contained many descendants of the original Creole inhabitants and large numbers of German, Irish, and Italian newcomers, almost all of the public schools were desegregated, and five of them contained seventy-five or more Negroes. The phenomenon, however, cannot be completely attributed to Latin toleration or immigrant aspirations. At least six schools were mixed in the "American" districts above Canal Street, the First and the Fourth, and the Fifth and Seventh Districts along the river below the city also contained integrated schools.[28]

The period from the spring of 1871 through the summer of 1874 was marked by tranquility and surprising white tolerance. The "peace and good order" reported by E. Warren Smith at the Bienville School seems to have been duplicated in most of the other desegregated schools. The conservative press, formerly vehement in its denunciation of school desegregation, for the most part turned very conciliatory. The *Daily Picayune* noted the reopening of the city schools in September, 1872, as "more encouraging and more satisfactory than in several years past," adding its belief that "altogether there are the strongest indications of the continued and deep affection of the people for our public school system." In June, 1873, the *Times* reported that the thoroughly desegregated Bienville School was "in fine condition morally, mentally and physically, and the discipline excellent."[29]

The politics of the Unification movement certainly played a prominent role in this new campaign for reconciliation. The elections of 1872 forced conservatives to realize that they had to break the Republican stranglehold on the black vote to oust the Radicals. To do this in New Orleans, where the crusade was centered,

---

were not desegregated until after 1874. In addition to these schools, testimony in the *Report of the Superintendent*, 1875, indicates that Clio, Hospital, and Jefferson schools might be added to Harlan's list.

28. Harlan, "Desegregation in New Orleans Schools," p. 667.

29. New Orleans *Daily Picayune*, Sept. 29, 1872; New Orleans *Times*, June 7, 1873.

they would have to convince a skeptical white citizenry that desegregated schools and public accommodations were indeed a
minor price to pay for the restoration of home rule. Enthusiastically supporting this venture, the *Picayune, Times,* and some of the
other Democratic dailies silenced their attacks on the public
schools and so contributed to an easing of racial animosities in
New Orleans.

The "era of good feeling," however, extended far deeper than
the pages of the press. This brief period of calm in a decade of
racial turbulence seems to have been characterized by a genuine
lessening of the tensions and hostilities which distinguished the
rest of the reconstruction. Public school administration policies
almost certainly contributed to the calm. During the 1872/73
academic year the pace of school desegregation slackened considerably. Negroes were steadily admitted into already mixed
schools, but few new targets were selected. Apparently the bolder
black parents had been able to place their children in the most
desirable schools during the first year and a half,[30] and the less
assertive parents who wanted their children in mixed schools
after 1872 chose to put them in facilities already adjusted to the
change.

This deceleration contributed to a noticeable diminution of
white animosities. In April, 1872, Reverend Thomas Markham
reported Presbyterian school enrollments "lessening in number
since the apprehension of admixture has subsided."[31] In September, 1872, the *Daily Picayune* noted that a sizeable number of
white students formerly enrolled in private schools were transferring back into the public schools.[32] This slowdown in new black

30. According to Harlan, "Desegregation in New Orleans Schools," p.
668, many of the integrated schools were considered to be among the best
in the public system. Bienville School, for example, placed more of its
graduates in the high schools in 1873 than any two other boys' schools
combined.
31. New Orleans *Southwestern Presbyterian,* Apr. 25, 1872.
32. New Orleans *Daily Picayune,* Sept. 29, 1872.

admissions apparently convinced many whites that the desegregation movement had run its course and that Negroes would be satisfied with the token gains they had achieved so far. When Judge Henry C. Dibble, now a school director for the Second Ward, approved the admission of some Negroes into the hitherto lily-white Webster School in April, 1873, the *Times* complained hotly: "It had been tacitly conceded by the best disposed of both races that the white and colored children should be kept apart in the schools. . . . During the year past the system was faithfully pursued and with the happiest results."[33] Although such new breakthroughs were uncommon, each one furnished fresh evidence that white frustration was merely dormant, not dead.

The peaceful progress toward public school desegregation was shattered suddenly and violently during the winter of 1874. In truth, the "era of good feeling" engendered by the Unification movement had deteriorated rapidly after the crusade was abandoned in July, 1873. Alarmed by the threat to white supremacy posed by Unification, segregationists revived some old "Democratic clubs" during the summer of 1873. They were organized into a new paramilitary structure known as the "White League," headed by New Orleanian Frederick Ogden, designated by one league member as "the first man of prominence to raise his voice against this proposed Covenant with Hell,"[34] Unification.

By the summer of 1874 it was becoming evident that the white supremacists were rapidly running out of patience. Republican rule was now in its seventh year in Louisiana, its appeal to whites not enhanced by its longevity. Throughout the country parishes all sorts of white leagues were forming for the purpose of intimidating black voters during the forthcoming political campaigns. In New Orleans Ogden's men spent the summer drilling

33. New Orleans *Times*, Apr. 10, 1873.
34. H. A. Vaught to John R. Ficklen, May 8, 1894, in the John R. Ficklen Papers, Louisiana State University Archives.

and parading up and down the city streets. On September 14, 1874, the New Orleans White League led an insurrection that momentarily deposed the Kellogg administration and proclaimed the return of Democratic sovereignty. For three days home rule was restored and "General" Ogden reigned unofficially as the military commandant of the city. The segregationists' coup d'etat collapsed, however, on September 17 after federal soldiers and three warships were summoned to New Orleans.[35]

Radical rule was temporarily preserved, but white anger and frustration did not diminish. Three months later the city again experienced an outbreak of white mob violence, directed on this occasion against the desegregated public schools. On December 14 a number of Negro girls from the Coliseum School, accompanied by a teacher, appeared to take entrance examinations at the lily-white Upper Girls' High School. Principal M. E. McDonald refused them admission, but, unable to control the resulting confusion, she excused a group of senior girls who had been practicing for their forthcoming graduation exercises. The girls regrouped in the school basement, where they drafted a resolution refusing to accept their diplomas "unless the question brought up this day . . . in regard to our school being mixed, is decided before the appointed time for our graduation." The girls of the junior and first-year classes followed suit, issuing a proclamation to the effect that they would boycott classes "until we are decisively informed whether the school is to be white or mixed."[36] Some black girls tried to enroll in the Lower Girls' High School on the same day, producing a similar reaction.[37]

35. Lonn, *Reconstruction in Louisiana*, pp. 256–59, 269–75.

36. Both quoted in the New Orleans *Daily Picayune*, Dec. 15, 1874, and the New Orleans *Bulletin*, Dec. 15, 1874. A superb eyewitness account by a member of the senior class is reprinted in Harris, *Education in Louisiana*, pp. 44–46. Although recalled a half century after the incident, the account is factually consistent with contemporary reports.

37. According to Harlan, "Desegregation in New Orleans Schools," p. 667, Lower Girls' High School was already desegregated at this time, so other factors may have accounted for the white boycott.

The high schools were commonly regarded by New Orleanians as the elite institutions in their public school system, especially Upper Girls'. Situated in a fashionable "uptown" neighborhood above Canal Street, Upper Girls' educated most of the young ladies of prestigious social connections in the public school system. In the four years that it had avoided desegregation, it had developed into something of a symbol of the larger controversy. Given the social priorities of white New Orleanians and the sexual connotations that permeated the race question, the attempt to desegregate Upper Girls' instigated a new round of civil disobedience.

After the Negro girls left the school, a large crowd of black men gathered in front of the building, allegedly yelling that they were "Tenth Ward niggers, and meant blood."[38] The next morning, when Superintendent Charles W. Boothby arrived at the school to investigate the disturbances, he was seized by a mob of white men and boys estimated at more than five hundred, threatened with lynching, and hauled to the office of the principal. A spokesman for the multitude handed him a prepared statement, awaiting his signature, committing him to exert himself "to prevent the occurrence of any event similar to that occurring in the Girls' High School, upper district, or in any school in this city, having reference to the mixture of white and colored pupils in the public schools."[39] According to one eyewitness, Boothby's "hand trembled so that he could scarcely write,"[40] but he managed to sign the statement and make his exit.

Boothby, whose latter-day conversion to racial segregation had been prompted by suggestions of the noose, was not the only prominent white Radical to begin to question the sagacity of integrated schools in the face of adversity. Henry C. Dibble, who had paved the way for desegregation as a judge and helped

38. New Orleans *Daily Picayune*, Dec. 15, 1874.
39. Quoted in the New Orleans *Daily Picayune*, Dec. 16, 1874, and the New Orleans *Bulletin*, Dec. 16, 1874.
40. Quoted in Harris, *Education in Louisiana*, p. 46.

put it into practice as a school board member, now proclaimed to a *Times* reporter that he had "long since been impressed with the danger to the whole public school system, were 'mixed schools' ... forced upon the people."[41] The New Orleans *Republican*, ever more concerned with Negro votes than Negro rights, hastened to applaud the stand taken by the high school girls, observing that "society would be more at peace and less exasperated against negro suffrage were the race relations reconciled by separation."[42]

These disclaimers failed to convince the black activists that surrender seemed the most sensible course. On the morning of December 17, some teen-aged Negro boys appeared at the Central Boys' High School and demanded admission. When angry white students barred their way, the youths summoned adult reinforcements and a battle developed. The students managed to fend off the outnumbered Negroes, but classes were abruptly dismissed by nervous school officials. The Central High boys, chided the day before by the *Bulletin* for failing to come to the aid of the high school girls, organized themselves into a vigilante committee to reinstitute the color line in the city schools. They went to the Lower Girls' High School and purged its student body of some twenty black girls. During the afternoon the Central High "regulators" visited a number of grammar schools, ousting the black students and warning them not to return.[43]

As the high school boys left the Keller School, where they had discovered and ejected two black children, they encountered their first resistance, a Negro gang made up of students from a nearby black school and a few adults. In the melee that followed an elderly Negro died, apparently the victim of a fall or heart attack. As word of the rioting and fatality spread, the mobs grew

41. New Orleans *Times*, Dec. 17, 1874.

42. New Orleans *Republican*, Dec. 17, 1874.

43. New Orleans *Bulletin*, Dec. 18, 1874; New Orleans *Daily Picayune*, Dec. 18, 1874; New Orleans *Republican*, Dec. 18, 1874; New Orleans *Times*, Dec. 18, 1874.

larger, until the whole Keller Market neighborhood was transformed into a battleground. Whites and blacks assaulted each other with stones, clubs, and bottles throughout the afternoon and into the evening. After several hours the teen-agers of both races retreated to their homes, leaving the neighborhood littered with rubble and broken glass. Rumors spread wildly throughout the city that blacks planned to burn down the Keller School and that whites would retaliate by setting fire to black schools. Bands of angry men—Negroes armed with fish knives, pistols, and razors and White Leaguers eager to renew the work of restoration interrupted by the federals three months earlier—patrolled the streets throughout the night. One White League platoon, allegedly fired upon from a Negro church on First and Freret, riddled the building with bullets, but none of the fleeing blacks was hit. Otherwise the night was quiet.[44]

On the following day the expulsion of black students from desegregated public schools continued. The Central High boys returned to the Lower Girls' High School to remove six Negroes overlooked the day before. Then the high schoolers abandoned their activities, but a mob of men and boys who had gathered to cheer them on visited several more grammar schools, ousting a number of black children from the Fillmore and St. Philip schools. In front of the Beauregard School, at the corner of Union and St. Claude, a group of armed Negroes dispersed the vigilantes by firing shots over their heads. These activities apparently inspired the white children in at least one grammar school to eject their black classmates.[45] None of these incidents, however, precipitated mayhem comparable to that exhibited on the streets near the Keller Market the day before.

With the weekend recess the uproar abated. The school board prudently closed down all of its schools a week ahead of schedule

44. *Ibid.*; New Orleans *Times*, Dec. 19, 1874.
45. New Orleans *Bulletin*, Dec. 19, 1874; New Orleans *Daily Picayune*, Dec. 19, 1874; New Orleans *Republican*, Dec. 19, 1874; New Orleans *Times*, Dec. 19, 1874.

for the Christmas vacation. With no integrated schools in session, the various vigilante squads disbanded. The *Times*, the *Picayune*, and even "General" Frederick Ogden urged a restoration of the peace.[46] It is obvious that the segregationist forces declared amnesty so readily because they were convinced that the color line in the city schools had been firmly restored. The *Republican* was urging such a policy, and even such notorious negrophiles as Superintendent Boothby and Judge Dibble had publicly recanted. On December 19 the school board announced its decision to reconsider the resegregation of its schools.[47] On the same day the *Times* laid the experiment to rest, asserting that the "revolution which was accomplished in the minds of the people long ago is now fully accomplished in fact.... There is no danger that mixed schools will be forced upon us here. That point is settled."[48]

The obituary proved rather premature, however, for the public schools reopened in January, 1875, as desegregated as they had been before the disturbances. The board of school directors voted on January 9 to resume classes without imposing racial changes. Anticipating further disruptions, it approved a resolution granting the board president and the city superintendent wide discretionary powers to close any or all of the schools instantly if further outbreaks of violence developed.[49] When classes resumed on January 11 with Negroes and whites still assigned to several of the same institutions, the disgruntled *Bulletin* spoke for many segregationists when it complained that it would be "better that every school be closed at once."[50]

A few black students returned to desegregated schools as soon

46. New Orleans *Daily Picayune*, Dec. 20, 1874; New Orleans *Times*, Dec. 19, 1874.

47. Reported in the New Orleans *Daily Picayune*, Dec. 20, 1874. The city school board minutes from June, 1869, through December, 1874, are not extant.

48. New Orleans *Times*, Dec. 19, 1874.

49. Orleans Parish School Board Minutes, Jan. 9, 1875.

50. New Orleans *Bulletin*, Jan. 13, 1875.

as classes began, but the majority of them cautiously decided to await further developments. In some institutions the aftereffects of the December disturbances were quite serious and long-lasting. In December, 1875, a full year later, the principal of the Jefferson School reported that the "spirit of disorder" had "spread throughout the school, and teachers had much labor and annoyance in restoring discipline." At the same time, officials at the Clio School reported attendance still substantially lower than it had been before the disruptions. At the Hospital School the principal noted that black attendance had been very poor following the violence, "the colored children being, as a rule, peculiarly susceptible to fear." But when it became apparent that no new disturbances were in the offing, most of the blacks originally enrolled in desegregated schools returned to their old classrooms. By the end of the year the Hospital School principal was able to report that "the panic then created has entirely subsided and its effects have totally disappeared."[51] In April, 1875, Superintendent Boothby reported to the school board that "the percentage of absence was unusually large during the months of January and February . . . produced by the violent attacks upon many of our schools in December," but noted that by March attendance levels had returned to a normal state.[52]

When it became apparent that the white protests would not be renewed, emboldened black activists returned to the offensive by challenging the color line at the very citadel of the December demonstrations, Central Boys' High School. On February 18, 1875, a young Negro named Roxborough showed up at the school with an order for admission authorized by school board officials requiring his placement in the senior class. After school authorities disclosed their helplessness to prevent Roxborough's admission, most of the seniors staged a walkout similar to the one

51. *Report of the Superintendent*, 1875, pp. 163–74.
52. Orleans Parish School Board Minutes, Apr. 7, 1875.

executed so successfully by the high school girls two months earlier. The maneuver failed to engender much excitement, however, partly because the sanctity of white womanhood was not at stake and partly because boycotts were becoming rather passé. Central High School remained desegregated, and integration soon spread to its faculty with the appointment of a mathematics teacher named E. J. Edmunds, a Paris-educated, *café au lait* Negro. Many of the walkouts never came back, but others eventually accepted the situation and resumed their studies.[53]

Despite the absence of renewed disruptions, school desegregation continued to rankle the white supremacists. When an alleged "shakedown" of teachers by school board officials was brought to light by the *Bulletin* in September, 1875, it brought about a heated protest replete with racial overtones. Prodded by the militantly segregationist *Bulletin*, the movement mushroomed into a gigantic public meeting held in Lafayette Square on September 29 to demand the resignations of most of the city school board members. A crowd estimated at nearly three thousand enthusiastically endorsed a resolution condemning the "compulsory admixture of children of all races, color and condition in the same schools, in the same rooms and on the same benches" as contrary to "the principles of humanity, repugnant to the instinct of both races, and . . . not required by any provision of the laws or Constitution of this State." Other resolutions condemned the appointment of the Negro Edmunds at Central High School and the conduct of the school board members, especially that of P. B. S. Pinchback, "the recognized leader of the colored members of the School Board, to force the race issue in the public schools."[54] The con-

53. New Orleans *Daily Picayune*, Feb. 19, 1875; New Orleans *Times*, Feb. 19, 20, 1875; Harris, *Education in Louisiana*, pp. 31, 46; Harlan, "Desegregation in New Orleans Schools," p. 667.

54. New Orleans *Bulletin*, Sept. 15, 1875; Orleans Parish School Board Minutes, Oct. 3, 1875; *Report of the Superintendent*, 1875, pp. 40–53; Harris, *Education in Louisiana*, p. 48.

troversy did not, however, engender enough anger to precipitate a renewal of the vigilante activities, and, as a result, school board personnel and policy remained unchanged.

If the white supremacists never lost their basic aversion to mixed schools throughout the reconstruction period, black activists and their white sympathizers never abandoned their indomitable determination to make the experiment work. Progress toward desegregation never again resumed its pre-1874 pace, but new inroads were made, causing in turn new manifestations of the ever-present tension between the races. At the Rampart Street School, where whites and Negroes had been enrolled together since 1872, officials had preserved peace by resorting to some of the same internal segregation devices utilized by twentieth-century diehards —separate classrooms, seating arrangements, and study groups. When the principal and first assistant moved toward real integration by abolishing these internal distinctions in November, 1875, their reforms resulted in an exodus of many of the white students.[55]

A longtime holdout was finally desegregated on September 18, 1876, when two black girls enrolled in the Paulding School. Both girls were driven away by some of the older boys, and when one of them pluckily returned on the following day she was repelled by mud and stones thrown by smaller boys. The incident was reported in the newspapers and apparently developed into a matter of honor for the black community, for a number of Negro parents showed up at the school with their children in tow on the morning of September 20, putting an end to the harassment.[56] This confrontation, occurring nearly six years after the first placement of black students in white schools,

55. New Orleans *Daily Picayune*, Nov. 10, 1875. None of the studies of the schools during this period mentions internal segregation, and official reports and contemporary accounts, with this one exception, ignore the subject. If such practices were commonly adopted, it would do much to account for the white toleration. This remains the most important unanswered question about the phenomenon.
56. New Orleans *Times*, Sept. 20, 21, 1876.

again attests to the singleminded stubbornness of both the Negro quest for equality and the white capacity for resistance.

Black students remained in predominantly white schools in New Orleans in fairly large numbers until the federal soldiers were withdrawn and the Radical Republican government collapsed in 1877. Black enrollment in the mixed schools, estimated between five hundred and one thousand before the disturbances of December, 1874, remained above three hundred from the riots to the very end. On the average, roughly five hundred black boys and girls were educated annually in anywhere from twenty-one to twenty-eight public schools with white classmates for a period of nearly seven years.

It must be remembered, however, that school desegregation remained the exception rather than the rule. If an average of five hundred Negroes attended integrated schools, nearly five thousand remained in separate institutions. It is likely that the percentage of white students who shared classrooms with Negroes was no higher. Several thousand whites attended private schools, and thousands of others were enrolled in public schools that escaped desegregation altogether. Many of the supposedly integrated schools were mixed only in a token way, with two or three blacks in one class and none in others. In some schools Negroes were segregated from whites by separate classrooms and other internal arrangements. Exact percentages cannot be computed, for school statistics during the period did not include analyses by race, but it may be assumed with relative certainty that no more than a small minority of whites and blacks studied side-by-side in the classrooms of the New Orleans public schools during the period from 1870 to 1877.

Public school desegregation in New Orleans lasted for seven years, but it never developed into more than a novelty sustained by the coalition of northerners and Negroes placed in power for a decade by the fortunes of war. Many white parents kept their children in the desegregated public schools because they could not afford tuition and would not deprive their sons and daughters of an education, but this resignation never mellowed into real acceptance of the situation. Only once did whites resort to widespread violence and intimidation, but the urge to do so never really abated. When the federal soldiers were withdrawn in 1877 and "home rule" was restored, the experiment was quickly laid to rest. Few of the mourners were white.

SEVEN

Jim Crow's Ascendancy

Radical reconstruction ended in Louisiana in April, 1877. On both the federal and state levels the elections of 1876 had developed into constitutional crises. At stake in Louisiana were the state's eight electoral votes, the governorship, and control of the legislature. While Congress debated the candidacies of Rutherford B. Hayes and Samuel Tilden, Republicans and Democrats in Louisiana each issued victory statements, inaugurated their state tickets, and convened their legislatures. Finally the "compromise of 1877," an eleventh-hour pact between Hayes aides and southern Bourbons, delivered the presidency to Hayes in return for various considerations, among them the promise to remove the federal soldiers from Louisiana and two other southern states. Hayes was inaugurated on March 4, 1877, and soon made public his intention to transfer the troops. On April 21 the Radical legislature disbanded, and three days later the occupational forces were ordered withdrawn. Twelve years and two weeks after Appomattox, the crusade to remold Louisiana in the image of its conquerors had finally run its course.[1]

1. For the presidential controversy, see C. Vann Woodward, *Reunion and Reaction: The Compromise of 1877 and the End of Reconstruction* (New York, 1951). Louisiana developments are discussed in Lonn, *Reconstruction in Louisiana*, pp. 400–525; William Ivy Hair, *Bourbonism and Agrarian Protest: Louisiana Politics, 1877–1900* (Baton Rouge, 1969), pp. 3–13; and Garnie W. McGinty, *Louisiana Redeemed: The Overthrow of Carpetbag Rule, 1876–1880* (New Orleans, 1941), pp. 25–151.

133

The race question was once again a central issue in the political campaign and its aftermath. The Republicans once again appealed for black votes by preaching racial equality, but this time the Democrats also made a concerted effort to win Negro support. Although a certain amount of intimidation and violence occurred in some of the country parishes, the Democrats, as William Ivy Hair put it, "began persuading Negro voters with parades instead of pistols, with beef barbecues rather than bullwhips."[2] During the campaign Democratic candidates and newspapers fondly recalled the ancient ties between master and slave, promising a future based upon harmony and mutual progress once the deceitful carpetbaggers were driven from the state. Even such a bigot as the White League editor of the Natchitoches *People's Vindicator* could offer "the right hand of fellowship" to the blacks, because "our interests are yours, yours are ours."[3] On the day that the Radical legislature dissolved itself, Governor Francis T. Nicholls promised to "obliterate the color line in politics and to consolidate the people on the basis of equal rights and common interests," and the Democratic legislature pledged to promote "kindly relations between the white and colored citizens of the State upon a basis of justice and mutual confidence."[4]

Some historians have suggested that the racial policies adopted by the "Redeemer" governments in the South after 1877 did not represent a drastic departure from those practiced by the Radicals they replaced. According to these scholars, the precise nature of the Negro's place in southern politics and society remained somewhat flexible until the Redeemers were in turn supplanted during the 1890s by the hard-line racists who initiated the orgy of Jim Crow legislation. Contending that the Reedeemers did not

2. Hair, *Bourbonism and Agrarian Protest*, p. 4.
3. Quoted in *ibid.*
4. Quoted in New Orleans *Republican*, Apr. 21, 1877.

"inaugurate any revolution in the customs and laws governing race relations," C. Vann Woodward has argued that their tenure was "a time of experiment, testing, and uncertainty."[5] Insisting that a "basic continuity existed between Radical and Redeemer rule" in Louisiana race relations, Henry C. Dethloff and Robert R. Jones have argued that the period from 1877 to 1898 was "a time of flux and experimentation" in regard to the Negro's station in Louisiana life.[6]

In truth, the Democratic Redeemers who came to power in Louisiana in 1877 were indeed divided on the question of the Negro's proper role in government and society. Many of them, including Lieutenant Governor Louis A. Wiltz and State Superintendent of Education Robert M. Lusher, were dogmatic white supremacists intent upon forcing the Negroes into a position as close to slavery as possible. Governor Nicholls, on the other hand, seems to have been imbued with a generous measure of paternalistic noblesse oblige. A planter-lawyer from Assumption Parish who lost an arm and a leg in the service of the Confederacy, Nicholls appointed a number of Negroes to minor public offices and spoke frequently of "kindness and strict justice to the colored people."[7] Nicholls seems to have belonged to that select class of patricians to whom, as Woodward has written, "Negro degradation was not a necessary corollary of white supremacy."[8] Throughout the 1880s and into the 1890s, this Democratic di-

5. C. Vann Woodward, *The Strange Career of Jim Crow*, 2d. rev. ed. (New York, 1966), p. 33.

6. Henry C. Dethloff and Robert R. Jones, "Race Relations in Louisiana, 1877–98," *Louisiana History*, IX (Fall, 1968), p. 304.

7. Quoted in Hair, *Bourbonism and Agrarian Protest*, p. 21.

8. Woodward, *Strange Career of Jim Crow*, p. 48. The classic presentation of this approach may be found in *ibid.*, pp. 47–59. For analyses of Nicholls' racial ideology, see Hair, *Bourbonism and Agrarian Protest*, pp. 20–23; Millard W. Warren, "A Study of Racial Views, Attitudes, and Relations in Louisiana, 1877–1902" (M.A. thesis, Louisiana State University, 1962), pp. 15–18; and C. Vann Woodward, *Origins of the New South, 1877–1913* (Baton Rouge, 1951), p. 209.

chotomy on the race question surfaced from time to time over such considerations as patronage, bargaining for the black vote, and appropriations for social services.

On one facet of race relations, however, the Louisiana Redeemers were neither ambivalent nor divided. Each of the Democratic leaders, including Nicholls, believed that the desegregation brought about under the Radicals, especially in the schools, had to be undone at once and the laws and guidelines sanctioning such policies negated as quickly as possible. On the subject of segregation in public facilities within their jurisdiction, Louisiana's new rulers exhibited scant sympathy for "experiment" or "testing." On the contrary, the Redeemers began to work toward a complete reversal of Radical policies in this area as soon as they took command.[9]

The public school system, long the primary battleground in the segregation struggle, was the natural place for the Redeemers to begin. During the 1876 campaign and the period of uncertainty that followed, the Democrats had been deliberately vague on the subject, hoping to attract black support without endangering their strength among the white voters. On April 20, 1877,

9. I do not mean to suggest, however, that the hypotheses advanced by Woodward, Dethloff, and Jones are not essentially valid in many respects. It is clear that Negroes retained a measure of political influence in Louisiana until they were disfranchised in 1898. Evidence suggests that the color line in some activities and public accommodations was less rigid during the 1880s than it later became. On the whole, Woodward, Dethloff, and Jones are most likely correct when they contend that Louisiana Negroes suffered more discrimination after 1898 than they did during the 1880s, although the exact degree of difference is open to debate. It is clear, however, that the alleged racial flexibility of the Democrats who took office in 1877 did not extend to the topic of integrated public facilities and that it required no revolution in party leadership to assure the enactment of Jim Crow legislation. After all, the man who signed the separate railroad coach bill into law as governor in 1890 and upheld its constitutionality as chief justice of the state supreme court in 1892 was none other than Francis T. Nicholls, widely acclaimed as the most liberal of the original Redeemers. On the issue of racial segregation the theme of continuity between Radicals and Redeemers in Louisiana race relations simply cannot be supported by the evidence.

Nicholls attempted to convince some of the Negroes in the dis-
integrating Radical legislature to take seats in the Democratic
assembly by advocating a system of public education in which
all children "without regard to race or color, may secure equal
advantages thereunder." On the same day the Democratic legislators issued a statement pledging a public school system "which
shall secure the education of white and colored citizens with
equal advantages."[10] Once they took office, however, the Redeemers soon made it clear that "equal advantages" did not include desegregated facilities.

Robert M. Lusher returned to the state superintendency of
public education, the post he had vacated in 1868 to take charge
of Peabody Fund operations in Louisiana. Undoing the work of
his two predecessors was not difficult. He began by using the
dictatorial appointive powers delegated to the office under Conway to purge local Republican school directors, replacing them
with Democrats known to be "safe" on the race issue. He then
replaced Conway's 1869 "rules and regulations" with a new set,
dropping the desegregation edict in favor of a directive that the
parish school boards "shall afford white and colored children,
respectively, equal facilities for their mental instruction and
moral training." In his annual report for 1877, Lusher rejoiced
that the "partisan rancor and blind fanaticism" responsible for
school desegregation "have now been dissipated by the sunlight
of peace and reconciliation." He reported that since his return
to the superintendency "parish directors have cheerfully opened
and liberally sustained a white and a colored school, apart, in
each ward, to the mutual satisfaction of both races."[11]

This "sunlight of peace and reconciliation" brought little
change to public education in the country parishes, where school
segregation had never been really challenged. In New Orleans,
however, where several hundred Negroes remained in predom-

10. Quoted in the New Orleans *Republican*, Apr. 21, 1877.
11. *Report of the Superintendent*, 1877, pp. iv-v, xiii.

inantly white public schools, the restoration of the Democrats led to sweeping changes in admission policies. On April 4, 1877, a Democratic school board took office, and former City Superintendent William O. Rogers returned to his old post after a seven-year stint in charge of the Presbyterian schools. One of the first actions initiated by the new officials was the authorization of belated diplomas for the high school seniors who had boycotted commencement ceremonies in December, 1874. In spite of their segregationist sympathies, however, they did not hasten to restore the color line at that time. Only a few weeks were left until the end of the term, and a majority of the school directors apparently felt that a wholesale reorganization would bring about unnecessary confusion. Already saddled with a number of financial and administrative difficulties, the Democratic board decided to defer racial readjustments until the beginning of the new term in September.[12]

To give an aura of objectivity to their plans, the directors authorized a special committee of three, headed by Archibald Mitchell, to investigate conditions in the desegregated city schools and to evaluate the results of the arrangement. The Mitchell report, submitted to the board on June 22, stated that the quality of public education in the city had "greatly deteriorated since colored and white children were admitted, indiscriminately, into the same schools." It offered examples of banishment of Negroes by force and white boycotts as evidence that desegregation had deprived students of both races of educational opportunities. It reported that "constant antagonism exhibited in quarrels, bickerings, and dissensions between pupils of different races" made the maintenance of discipline impossible in desegregated classrooms. On the basis of these findings, the committee recommended that whites and Negroes be placed in separate schools. The board endorsed the Mitchell report on July 3 and authorized Superintendent Rogers to apportion the schools be-

12. Orleans Parish School Board Minutes, Apr. 4, 18, 1877.

fore the September reopening. Rogers submitted a blueprint for racial reorganization on August 1, allocating thirty-seven of the schools to the whites and twenty-two to the Negroes.[13]

The plan did not unfold as smoothly in practice. In spite of a directive ordering all personnel to limit black students to the twenty-two designated schools, an estimated three hundred Negroes were allowed to return to integrated classrooms in September, forcing Rogers and his deputies to ferret them out on a school-by-school basis. On December 5, Rogers was able to report that the "separation of the white and colored pupils has been made in all the schools—except in the Rampart and Bayou Road, where the changes are still in progress."[14] During the Christmas recess the last black holdouts were reassigned to Negro schools, bringing to an end a truly unique experiment in interracial coexistence.

Many black activists were unwilling to surrender without a struggle. Soon after the school board announced its plans, a delegation of New Orleans Negroes led by the aged patriarch Aristide Mary, called upon Governor Nicholls to seek his intercession. The blacks angrily denounced the reorganization of the public schools and demanded that the governor fulfill his campaign pledges to uphold Negro rights. Nicholls reiterated his promise that black children would be given "equal facilities all through, both in teachers, buildings and books," but insisted that his commitment to equal facilities had never been intended as an endorsement of mixed classrooms. Arguing that whites would not attend desegregated schools, Nicholls refused to sanction a system of public education beneficial to the blacks alone. "If you believe there has been a violation of the constitution," he reportedly told the delegation, "the courts are open and there lies your redress."[15]

One New Orleans Negro who decided to accept Nicholls'

13. *Ibid.*, June 22, July 3, Aug. 1, 1877.
14. *Ibid.*, Dec. 5, 1877; New Orleans *Daily Picayune*, Dec. 6, 1877.
15. Quoted in the New Orleans *Daily Picayune*, June 27, 1877.

challenge was Paul Trevigne, former editor of the defunct *L'Union* and a member of the recently deposed Radical school board. On September 26, 1877, Trevigne appeared in Sixth District Court to seek an injunction against Superintendent Rogers and the new board of school directors restraining them from proceeding with their plan to restore the color line in the public schools. According to Trevigne, Rogers and the school board were violating the Fourteenth Amendment of the U.S. Constitution and Article 135 of the state constitution by a policy "which works an irreparable injury to the entire colored population of the city in that it tends to degrade them as citizens by discriminating against them on account of race and color."[16] On the evening of September 27, a mass meeting was held on Common Street to demonstrate black support for the litigation. Resolutions were resoundingly approved condemning the school reorganization as discriminatory, unconstitutional, and a rank betrayal of Democratic campaign promises. When Trevigne announced that he intended to pursue his fight to the limits of the law, the crowd roared its approval and a number of well-to-do Negroes pledged contributions to help underwrite his legal expenses.[17]

The Trevigne suit placed new Sixth District Judge N. H. Rightor in a rather difficult position. As a judge, he was obligated to uphold a state constitution which plainly prohibited "separate schools or institutions of learning established exclusively for any race by the state of Louisiana." As a white Democrat, he was personally and politically committed to racial segregation. Rightor solved his dilemma by seizing upon two technicalities to deny the injunction without handing down a ruling on the constitutional questions at issue. On October 23, 1877, he dismissed Trevigne's request on the grounds that it had been filed too late for the board to reverse its policy and that the plantiff had demon-

16. New Orleans *Times*, Sept. 27, 1877.
17. *Ibid.*, Sept. 28, 1877.

strated no personal injury as a result of the school reorganization.[18]

Black strategists apparently anticipated this exigency, for another New Orleans Negro, Arnold Bartonneau, immediately
filed suit against the city school board, Rogers, and George H.
Gordon, principal of the Fillmore School, accusing them of con-
spiring to violate his civil rights by denying his children admission to the public school closest to their home. As Trevigne had
done, Bartonneau argued that the public school reorganization
was in violation of the Fourteenth Amendment and Article 135.
Unlike Trevigne, however, Bartonneau was able to buttress his
case with evidence that the actions of the defendants had brought
about personal inconvenience and injury.[19]

The case of *Bartonneau* v. *New Orleans Board of School Directors et al.* was finally decided on February 19, 1879. In a decision very similar to that set forth by the Supreme Court in
Plessy v. *Ferguson* seventeen years later, United States Circuit
Judge W. B. Woods dismissed the suit, ruling that Bartonneau
had not proved that the defendants had prevented his children
from securing a public education or that they had forced the
children into facilities that were necessarily inferior to those
provided for whites. According to Woods: "Both races are
treated precisely alike. White children and colored children are
compelled to attend different schools. That is all. The State, while
conceding equal privileges and advantages to both races, has the
right to manage its schools in the manner which in its judgement
will best promote the interest of all."[20] As the jubilant *Daily Picayune* exulted, "Judge Woods has swept away every obstacle to
the successful workings of our school system that political and
social theorizers have attempted to set up."[21]

18. *Ibid.*, Oct. 24, 1877.
19. *Ibid.*
20. Quoted in the New Orleans *Daily Picayune*, Feb. 20, 1879.
21. *Ibid.*, Feb. 21, 1879.

During the Radical reign, a few New Orleans Negroes had tested the state and federal public accommodations laws and had won admission to such facilities as white theatre boxes and saloons. The Redeemers evidently worried less about desegregated accommodations than mixed schools, for they made no effort to raise the issue upon their accession to office. Nevertheless, their ideas on the matter are no mystery. On the day that the Republican legislature disbanded in April, 1877, a black barber named Joe Craig, founder of a "colored conservative club" and a recently appointed school director, tried to take a seat among some white Democrats celebrating in the rotunda of the St. Charles Hotel. His treatment was symbolic of the new order—he was pitched bodily into the street.[22] The courts were now in Democratic hands, lessening chances that Negroes would be able to gain redress for such wrongs, but a substantial body of state and federal antidiscrimination legislation remained on the books. Before the color line in places of public accommodation could be made totally secure, such enactments as Article Thirteen of the state constitution, the Louisiana civil rights laws of 1869 and 1873, and the federal Civil Rights Act of 1875 had to be revoked or invalidated.

In January, 1878, the United States Supreme Court set the process in motion with its decision in the case of *Hall* v. *De Cuir*. In 1875 a black woman named Josephine De Cuir tried to secure a cabin on the steamboat *Governor Allen* for a trip from New Orleans upriver to Hermitage, a landing on the Louisiana bank of the Mississippi. When her request was rejected by John G. Benson, owner and captain of the vessel, Mrs. De Cuir brought suit against Benson in Eighth District Court in New Orleans. Assuming that the journey in question had been intrastate in nature, Mrs. De Cuir based her action upon the Louisiana Civil Rights Act of 1869, which prohibited racial segregation on com-

22. New Orleans *Republican*, Apr. 21, 1877.

mon carriers operating within the boundaries of the state. Mrs. De Cuir was awarded one thousand dollars, and the Louisiana State Supreme Court upheld the ruling.

During the litigation Captain Benson died, but the case was appealed to the United States Supreme Court by his administratrix, Eliza Jane Hall. On January 14, 1879, the Supreme Court reversed the decision and declared the state law unconstitutional. In the majority opinion, Chief Justice Morrison R. Waite ruled that the Mississippi River was an interstate waterway under the jurisdiction of the Congress and that Mrs. De Cuir's voyage, even though it began and ended in Louisiana, was therefore interstate in nature. Because the state law in question failed to differentiate adequately between intrastate and interstate commerce, it was declared null and void.[23] By implication, the high court's ruling also invalidated the untested state Civil Rights Act of 1873, which expressly claimed jurisdiction over interstate carriers operating in Louisiana.

This decision left the public accommodations and public school provisions of the 1868 constitution as the last remaining desegregation decrees in force at the state level. In his annual report for 1877, State Superintendent Lusher had denounced Articles 135 and 136 as "offensive provisions" and urged the legislature to permit "no delay in replacing these articles by more acceptable provisions for the mental instruction and moral training of the two races, in separate schools."[24] Lusher was not the only segregationist seeking constitutional change. In September, 1877, the militantly white supremacist Opelousas *Courier* began to marshal support for a new convention. By January, 1878, the *Courier* reported that twenty-seven journals throughout Louisiana had endorsed its stand, including such powerful Democratic newspapers as the Baton Rouge *Advocate*, the Monroe *Ouachita*

23. *Hall* v. *De Cuir*, 93 U.S. (1878).
24. *Report of the Superintendent*, 1877, pp. iv-v.

Telegraph, the Shreveport *Times*, and the New Orleans *Daily Picayune*.[25]

The safety of segregation was by no means the only issue involved in the convention controversy, nor was it even the principal consideration. Anti-Nicholls Democrats, headed by Lieutenant Governor Louis A. Wiltz, were plotting to shorten the governor's term by overhauling the election laws.[26] In addition, the labyrinthine controversy encompassed such considerations as relocation of the state capital, state debt revision, levee taxation, and a new charter for the infamous Louisiana Lottery Company. Proponents soft-pedaled the race issue, hoping to avert unwanted scrutiny from Republicans in Washington, but there can be little doubt that it was an important factor in their urgency for constitutional revision. In January, 1879, Nicholls reluctantly signed into law a bill calling for elections to select delegates to undo the work of the "black and tan" constitution of 1868.[27]

The Democrats captured nearly three-fourths of the seats and controlled the convention from the opening gavel on April 21 through adjournment on July 23. Despite the segregationist leanings of the Democratic majority, the constitution of 1879 was almost altogether mute on the subject. It must be remembered that the Fourteenth Amendment expressly outlawed racial discrimination imposed by a state, and the delegates were not certain how far the federal courts would go toward its enforcement. The Civil Rights Act of 1875 specifically prohibited racial segregation in certain areas of public accommodation, and the Democratic delegates did not want to jeopardize their handiwork by provoking a direct confrontation with federal law. So the delegates simply achieved constitutional change by silence. Gone

25. Opelousas *Courier*, Sept. 1, 8, 1877; Jan. 18, 1878.
26. Much of this opposition stemmed from Nicholls' appointment of Negroes to public positions and other manifestations of what one opposition newspaper branded "rampant pseudoliberalism."
27. McGinty, *Louisiana Redeemed*, pp. 154–59; Hair, *Bourbonism and Agrarian Protest*, pp. 89, 99–104.

from the new "bill of rights" was the ban on segregated places of public accommodation; gone from the oath of office was the pledge to uphold racial equality; gone from the section on public education was the enjoinder against "separate schools or institutions of learning established exclusively for any race by the State of Louisiana."[28]

Only once did the delegates overtly write racial distinction into the new document. Article 231 authorized "a university for the education of persons of color" to be situated in New Orleans.[29] Louisiana State University, starved to the brink of extinction during the Kellogg administration because of its lily-white admissions policy, was once again safely segregated, a development that left Louisiana Negroes without a comparable opportunity for public higher education. In other words, Article 231 did not bring about segregation; it merely transformed a policy of total ostracism into one of the "separate but equal" variety. In 1880 Southern University opened its doors in New Orleans.[30]

After the voters adopted the new constitution in December, 1879, the federal Civil Rights Act of 1875 stood as the last legal impediment to segregation in Louisiana. This edict had been ignored for the most part in New Orleans after 1877, but as late as the summer of 1881 the New Orleans *Weekly Louisianian* reported that Lake Pontchartrain's bathhouses and picnic grounds were not segregated and at least one lakefront saloon made a practice of catering to thirsty whites and Negroes alike.[31] Unique in New Orleans, integrated facilities were virtually nonexistent in the country parishes, where local blacks had made no real ef-

28. *Constitution of the State of Louisiana, Adopted in Convention at the City of New Orleans, July 23, 1879* (New Orleans, 1879), pp. 3–5, 41, 56–58.
29. *Ibid.*, p. 58.
30. *Acts of Louisiana*, 1880, no. 87.
31. New Orleans *Weekly Louisianian*, June 19, 1880; June 25, July 23, 1881; Dorothy Rose Eagleson, "Some Aspects of the Social Life of the New Orleans Negro in the 1880s" (M.A. thesis, Tulane University, 1961), p. 102.

fort to test the various accommodations laws. In May, 1882, T. T. Allain, a prominent black legislator influential in securing federal levee funds for the state just a month before, was taken into the Sumter House Bar in Baton Rouge by John Hill, a wealthy white planter from West Baton Rouge Parish. Despite the political implications, the white invitation, and the Sumner law, Allain was unceremoniously thrown out of the tavern.[32]

In October, 1883, Louisiana segregationists were again assisted by the United States Supreme Court. In *Civil Rights Cases*, a collective ruling on five separate suits, the Court invalidated the Civil Rights Act of 1875. The majority opinion, written by Justice Joseph P. Bradley, asserted that the measure was justified by neither the Thirteenth nor the Fourteenth Amendment. According to Bradley, the jurisdiction of the Fourteenth Amendment did not include arrangements between private parties. Moreover, he contended, it "would be running the slavery argument into the ground" to apply the Thirteenth Amendment to "every act of discrimination which a person may see fit to make as to the guests he will entertain, or as to the people he will take into his coach or cab or car, or admit to his concert or theatre, or deal with in other matters of intercourse or business."[33] Despite an eloquent dissent written by Justice John Marshall Harlan, the decision struck down the last of the desegregation laws under which Louisiana Negroes had fought to free themselves from the humiliation of the color line.

Louisiana Democrats waited seven more years to concoct the first of many Jim Crow laws, but they were already busy systematically separating the races in all public facilities directly under their control. After Southern University was authorized by Ar-

32. Warren, "Racial Views, Attitudes, and Relations," pp. 47–48; Dethloff and Jones, "Race Relations in Louisiana," p. 312. The latter study cites the incident as evidence of racial flexibility, arguing, "One looks in vain for examples of white men who would even consider socializing with Negroes in polite society after the advent of Jim Crow."
33. *Civil Rights Cases*, 109 U.S. (1883).

ticle 231 of the constitution of 1879, every new public institution of higher learning chartered was born with racial designations. In 1884 the Louisiana State Normal School at Natchitoches was opened "to white persons of either sex." Ten years later the legislature authorized the Louisiana Polytechnic Institute in Ruston for "the education of the white children of the State of Louisiana in the arts and sciences." In 1898 Southwestern Louisiana Industrial Institute was established in Lafayette for "the education of the white children of the State of Louisiana."[34]

Similar patterns occurred in other state facilities. The Charity Hospital of Louisiana, in New Orleans, had been segregated before the Civil War, a practice which was probably continued through reconstruction as well. After 1877 the separation grew steadily more systematic. The annual report for 1880 recommended two new Negro wards to satisfy "the largely increasing demand for admission by the colored population." In 1882 the venereal disease department was reduced to make room for another black surgical ward. By 1884 ten of fifty-two wards were being used by Negro patients. Black men were quartered in three medical and three surgical wards, and black women occupied four wards, one each for obstetric, surgical, medical, and gynaecological purposes.[35]

The state mental hospital in Jackson experienced similar developments. No separate facilities had been set apart for black patients before the Civil War, primarily because so few Negroes had been admitted that they were simply quartered in three or four separate cells. But black admissions escalated sharply during the reconstruction. By the end of 1877, of the 194 patients in the asylum, 59 were Negroes. In the annual report for that year, the newly appointed Democratic board of trustees recommended "appropriate provision . . . for the separation of the classes."[36] By

34. *Acts of Louisiana*, 1884, no. 51; 1894, no. 68; 1898, no. 162.
35. *Report, Charity Hospital*, 1880, p. 7; 1882, p. 7; 1884, p. 29.
36. *Report, Insane Asylum*, 1877, pp. 15, 18.

1882 whites and Negroes were eating in separate dining rooms. Segregated dormitories followed two years later.[37] In 1902, when the legislature approved creation of the Colored Asylum of the State of Louisiana at Pineville, the Democrats achieved the ultimate method of preserving the priorities of race among the mentally ill.[38]

The segregationist impulse in Louisiana was not limited to native Democrats or former Confederates. A state chapter of the Grand Army of the Republic, organized in 1883 by white Union veterans then living in Louisiana, adamantly refused to accept black veterans into its ranks despite strong pressure from the national organization. During a factional dispute in 1889, State Commander Jacob Gray set up several black posts with a total membership of more than seven hundred, an action that tore the chapter apart. Bitter whites complained in 1891 that the "inexorable law of the social condition is such that the white man who associates upon terms of social equality with a black man is barred from all association with the people of the white race."[39] After two state commanders were dismissed by national officials for refusing to recognize the Negro posts, the whites abandoned the G.A.R. rather than accept the social stigma of integration.[40]

During the 1880s and into the 1890s a few organizations, facilities, and activities operated without rigid systems of racial segregation. An estimated 75,000 black Roman Catholics still went to church with whites, although they were seated in separate sections and were required to receive Holy Communion after the whites. Certain varieties of athletic activity defied the color line

37. Wisner, *Public Welfare Administration*, p. 107; *Journal of the House*, 1884, p. 306; Dethloff and Jones, "Race Relations in Louisiana," pp. 313–14.

38. *Acts of Louisiana*, 1902, no. 92.

39. Grand Army of the Republic, Department of Louisiana and Mississippi, *Proceedings of the Eighth Annual Encampment, 1891* (New Orleans, 1891), p. 16.

40. Wallace E. Davies, "Segregation in the G.A.R.," *Journal of Southern History*, XIII (Aug., 1947), pp. 354–72.

in New Orleans, as did some of the city's brothels. Although rail-roads operating in Louisiana commonly provided Jim Crow coaches during the 1880s, some lines apparently allowed black passengers to share depot facilities, restrooms, and first-class cars with whites. Negroes continued to ride on any New Orleans streetcar and to sit where they pleased, though they tended to take seats in the rear of the cars as a general rule.[41] Not one of these areas of interracial contact, however, survived the mount-ing pressure for color-line conformity during the fin de siècle years.

The division of the Roman Catholic church in Louisiana into separate parishes was not altogether the result of Jim Crow en-thusiasm, although the desire for lily-white churches provided much of the impetus. Archbishop Francis Janssens, a Dutch-born prelate placed in charge of the Archdiocese of New Orleans in 1888, believed that many black Catholics were deserting the church in disgust over white bigotry and their lack of a voice in parish affairs. In 1895 Janssens created a "national church" for Louisiana Negroes under the aegis of the Assumptionist Fathers. Despite the bitter opposition of many black Catholics, who viewed the arrangement as outright ostracism, segregated par-ishes soon became a reality for all Louisiana Catholics.[42]

During this period Jim Crow also spread to certain athletic activities in New Orleans. Negroes had never participated in such genteel white sports as cycling and tennis, but for a genera-tion after Appomattox they competed against whites on the race tracks, in the boxing rings, and on the baseball diamonds of the city. White baseball teams frequently played exhibition games against such black nines as the "Bostons" and the "Pickwicks," made up of employees of those exclusive white clubs. These inter-racial contests often drew crowds "composed of the best elements

41. Dethloff and Jones, "Race Relations in Louisiana," pp. 312, 314–15.
42. For a comprehensive study of this development, see Dolores Egger Labbé, *Jim Crow Comes to Church: The Establishment of Segregated Catholic Parishes in South Louisiana* (Lafayette, La., 1971).

of both colors," according to one source. During the same period black jockeys often rode against whites in the horse races held on the Fair Grounds and Metairie ovals. Mixed boxing matches were not uncommon. Andy Bowen, a local Negro nicknamed "the Louisiana Tornado," was one of the toughest lightweights in the United States and a popular New Orleans ring attraction. In 1886 Bowen fought and defeated James Farrell, a white lightweight from Pittsburgh, and the white crowd reportedly hailed the decision with "cheers for upholding the honor of New Orleans muscle." Bowen continued to box against white opponents in New Orleans until 1891.[43]

The color line in these sports developed during the 1880s and early 1890s. In July, 1885, a scheduled baseball game between a black team and a white squad drew heated protests from other white teams, who threatened to boycott games against the offending white nine. This tempest prompted the *Daily Picayune* to predict that any white team daring to compete against blacks "will have to brave considerable opposition on the part of the other clubs." By 1890 desegregated baseball games were no longer held, and black jockeys had been banished from the local tracks. The last interracial boxing match staged in the city was a bout between George "Little Chocolate" Dixon, a Boston Negro, and "Irish Jack" Skelly on September 6, 1892. Black spectators were allowed into the Olympic Club for the first time. This innovation, compounded by the savage beating Dixon inflicted upon his white adversary, seems to have outraged the racial sensibilities of many New Orleans whites. The *Times-Democrat* complained that it had been "a mistake to match a negro and a white man, a mistake to bring the races together on any terms of equality, even in the prize ring." A few days later the *Picayune* re-

43. New Orleans *Daily Picayune*, Feb. 1, 1886; Nov. 5, 1888; Dale A. Somers, *The Rise of Sports in New Orleans* (Baton Rouge, 1972), pp. 96–97, 120–21, 181–83, 286–90.

ported that the Olympic Club had agreed to allow "no more matches to be fought there, which ignore or disregard the color line." With that announcement, mixed athletic competition ended in New Orleans.[44]

During this period rigid segregation also spread to New Orleans prostitution, though the women "notoriously abandoned to lewdness" were considerably slower to embrace Jim Crow than were citizens engaged in more pristine pursuits. Throughout the 1880s a few white harlots sold their favors to black customers. Some plainly preferred Negroes and supported black "fancy men." On November 30, 1889, the *Mascot*, a weekly tabloid specializing in red-light gossip, charged that "this thing of white girls becoming enamored of negroes is becoming rather too common."[45] A few brothels with black and white prostitutes continued to operate in the squalid sin district along Dauphine and Burgundy Streets during the 1880s, but they were the last of a rapidly vanishing institution. By that time virtually all of the whorehouses in New Orleans were totally white or totally black, from the elegant Basin Street palaces to the fifteen-cent Negro cribs along "Smoky Row" on Burgundy between Conti and Bienville. When the city fathers established the famous Storyville district in 1897, they prohibited racially mixed houses in the area.[46]

The state legislature was by no means immune to the Jim Crow enthusiasm. It waited for seven years after the Supreme Court nullified the Sumner law to begin writing "separate but equal" into Louisiana law, but the delay must be attributed to constitutional uncertainty, not to any reluctance on the part of the Democratic majority. In March, 1890, the Supreme Court sanc-

44. New Orleans *Daily Picayune*, July 4, 1885; Sept. 11, 1892; New Orleans *Times-Democrat*, Sept. 8, 1892; Somers, *Rise of Sports*, pp. 120–21, 181–83, 286–90.
45. Quoted in Asbury, *The French Quarter*, p. 388.
46. *Ibid.*, pp. 350–94, 424–55.

tioned a Mississippi law requiring separate railroad cars for white and black passengers.[47] Two months later a similar measure was put before the Louisiana legislature. Demanding that every railroad operating in the state "provide equal but separate accommodations for the white, and colored races, by providing two or more passenger coaches . . . or by dividing the passenger coaches by a partition," the bill set penalties for violators and granted the railroads immunity from lawsuits arising from its enforcement.[48]

This legislation engendered the last real black protest activity in nineteenth-century Louisiana. Since 1877 many Negroes had raged inwardly over a social code that increasingly required them to "sit in the cockloft of a theatre or stay at home."[49] The separate coach proposal became a catalyst transforming this discontent into one final confrontation with the minions of Jim Crow. The New Orleans *Crusader*, a weekly newspaper founded in 1889 by the militant Louis A. Martinet, tried to rekindle the fighting spirit of the city's black community. The Louisiana chapter of the American Citizens' Equal Rights Association sent a memorial to the legislature, signed by Martinet, P. B. S. Pinchback, Paul Trevigne, the ancient Aristide Mary, and thirteen others, denouncing the proposal as "a free license to the evilly-disposed that they might with impunity insult, humiliate and otherwise maltreat innocent persons . . . who should happen to have a dark skin."[50] Many of the eighteen black legislators spoke against the bill, including C. F. Brown, who called it "a disgrace to any State

47. *Louisville, New Orleans, and Texas Railroad* v. *Mississippi*, 133 U.S. 587 (1889).

48. *Acts of Louisiana*, 1890, no. 111.

49. "Justice" to George W. Cable, Feb. 24, 1887, in the George W. Cable Papers, Tulane University Archives.

50. *Journal of the House*, 1890, pp. 127–28, reprinted in Otto H. Olsen, ed., *The Thin Disguise: The Turning Point in Negro History, Plessy v. Ferguson* (New York, 1968), pp. 47–50. Olsen's introduction to this collection of documents, correspondence, and editorials pertaining to *Plessy v. Ferguson* contains many excellent insights into Louisiana race relations, especially from a black perspective.

in the Union," and Victor Rochon, who accused its sponsors of casting "the odium of pariahism upon the colored people of this State."[51]

This criticism, however, had little effect upon the white lawmakers, who apparently agreed with the *Times-Democrat* that a white man who "would be horrified at the idea of his wife or daughter seated by the side of a burly negro in the parlor of a hotel or at a restaurant cannot see her occupying a crowded seat in a car next to a negro without the same feeling of disgust."[52] The black legislators did win a momentary victory by threatening to oppose a lottery bill, but once that measure was safely passed the separate car proposal was quickly adopted by the senate and signed into law by Governor Nicholls.[53]

Undaunted by this turn of events, Martinet and other activists began to prepare a legal challenge, counseled by the eminent white egalitarian Albion W. Tourgée. On September 1, 1891, Aristide Mary, Martinet, and others met in New Orleans to set up the Citizens' Committee to Test the Constitutionality of the Separate Car Law and to coordinate strategy. Their initial attempt failed to develop into a test case, but the second was more productive. On June 7, 1892, a Negro named Homer Plessy boarded a Covington-bound East Louisiana Railroad train in New Orleans and took a seat in the white coach. When he refused to move to the Jim Crow car, he was removed from the train and placed under arrest. When Plessy was found guilty by Orleans Parish Judge John H. Ferguson, his attorneys appealed the case to the state supreme court. When that panel upheld the conviction, they proceeded toward their ultimate objective, a

51. *Journal of the House*, 1890, pp. 202–3, reprinted in Olsen, *The Thin Disguise*, pp. 50–52.

52. New Orleans *Times-Democrat*, July 9, 1890, reprinted in Olsen, *The Thin Disguise*, pp. 52–54.

53. Olsen, *The Thin Disguise*, pp. 9–11. Nicholls, who apparently learned during his first term as governor that even his timorous brand of racial paternalism was politically dangerous in Louisiana, proved much more orthodox during his second term.

hearing before the United States Supreme Court. Finally, in May, 1896, the Court put an end to their quest with its infamous decision that Fourteenth Amendment guarantees of equal protection of the laws were not abridged by what John Marshall Harlan termed "the thin disguise of 'equal' accommodations."[54]

Plessy v. *Ferguson* removed the last fragile restraints from the Louisiana white supremacists. In 1894, while the case was still in litigation, the state legislature adopted two more Jim Crow bills, one expanding railway segregation to depot waiting rooms and the other prohibiting racially mixed marriages in Louisiana. A new state constitution approved in 1898 expressly required segregated public schools and, in effect, placed "white only" signs on Louisiana ballot boxes by enacting new property and literacy qualifications. Four years later the legislature laid to rest the last remaining evidence of the black power movement during reconstruction when it adopted a bill requiring the separation of white and black passengers on New Orleans streetcars. Within a few years the "equal but separate" arrangement was applied by state law to even more facilities and activities, including boarding houses, jails, circus and tent-show entrances, and even extra-marital love affairs.[55]

The proud black people of Louisiana found it necessary to submit to these humiliations, not because the vast majority of them were "apathetic or inarticulate, or both,"[56] as one study has claimed, but because every possible alternative to submission had been taken from them. Negroes could no longer work through the political process. They could not expect redress from a federal judiciary capable of such reactionary decisions as *Plessy* v.

54. *Plessy* v. *Ferguson*, 163 U.S. 537 (1896); Olsen, *The Thin Disguise,* pp. 11–17, 69–121; Barton J. Bernstein, "*Plessy* v. *Ferguson*: Conservative Sociological Jurisprudence," *Journal of Negro History,* XLVIII (July, 1963), pp. 192–98.

55. *Acts of Louisiana*, 1894, no. 54, no. 98; 1902, no. 64; 1908, no. 87; 1914, no. 235; 1918, no. 258; 1921, no. 106.

56. Dethloff and Jones, "Race Relations in Louisiana," p. 319.

Ferguson and *Williams* v. *Mississippi*.[57] They did not command the economic leverage to stage successful boycotts. The ultimate alternative, protest through physical resistance, would have been suicidal at a time when white violence was assuming epidemic proportions and legal authorities were putting forth little effort to bring to justice those guilty of applied genocide.[58]

The plight of the Negroes was compounded by the fact that only one prominent white Louisianian raised his voice on their behalf after 1877. George W. Cable, born and raised in New Orleans, the city he portrayed so fondly in his stories of Creole life, began his crusade for equal justice in 1875 by composing a letter published in the *Bulletin* supporting desegregated public schools. After 1877 he grew increasingly disturbed by the spread of segregation and other forms of racial discrimination. In hundreds of public lectures and works such as "The Freedman's Case in Equity" (1884), *The Silent South* (1885), and *The Negro Question* (1890), Cable argued eloquently that the white people of the South would never enjoy responsible government, liberty, and justice so long as they denied them to Negroes.[59]

These unorthodox opinions subjected Cable to a torrent of vitriolic abuse throughout the South, spearheaded in New Orleans by Page Baker, editor of the *Times-Democrat*, and the aged Creole historian Charles Etienne Gayarré. Typical was Gayarré's declaration that Cable harbored the desire to sink the white race "socially, civilly, and politically below the black race, which he

57. *Williams* v. *Mississippi*, 170 U.S. 213 (1898), was the decision that sanctioned Negro disfranchisement by upholding the constitutionality of Mississippi poll tax and literacy requirements.

58. Hair, *Bourbonism and Agrarian Protest*, pp. 182–85, 186–90.

59. Arlin Turner, *George W. Cable: A Biography* (Durham, 1956), pp. 194–262. Other interpretations of Cable's racial ideology can be found in Woodward, *Strange Career of Jim Crow*, pp. 45–46, and Lawrence J. Friedman, *The White Savage: Racial Fantasies in the Postbellum South* (Englewood Cliffs, N.J., 1970), pp. 99–117. A convenient anthology of Cable's writings on the subject is Arlin Turner, ed., *The Negro Question: A Selection of Writings on Civil Rights in the South by George W. Cable* (Garden City, N.Y., 1958).

considers superior to ours and destined to africanize the entire south."[60] Vilified in his own home town as a traitor to his race and region and "as deprived of all moral sense as the crocodile,"[61] Cable was eventually driven into exile in New England, prey to what W. J. Cash described as the "savage ideal," a state of mental tyranny "whereunder dissent and variety are completely suppressed and men become, in all their attitudes, professions, and actions, virtual replicas of one another."[62]

Scholars have provided many explanations for the South's capitulation to such rabid racism during this period. In *The Strange Career of Jim Crow*, C. Vann Woodward has argued that the triumph of the extreme bigots was caused in large part by national and regional developments after 1877—the abandonment of the Negroes by northern Republicans, the demise of the paternalistic Redeemers, and the bitter political divisions engendered by the Populist crusade.[63] Although the Redeemer commitment to Negro rights was largely illusory in Louisiana, the other developments cited by Woodward were certainly factors in the ascendancy of Jim Crow in the state. Without the acquiescence of many northern Republicans and the outright cooperation of Republican justices, the Louisiana legislators would have been intimidated or their handiwork invalidated. The chicanery and fraud involving manipulation of the black vote in the Populist-Bourbon campaigns of 1894 and 1896 undoubtedly helped pave the way for Negro disfranchisement in 1898.

This explanation, however, fails to take into account a factor of fundamental importance in the development of the Jim Crow phenomenon in Louisiana—the unusual desperation of the struggle to determine the Negro's "place" during the reconstruction.

60. Charles Gayarré, "Revue des Grandissimes," *Le Propagateur Catholique*, Dec. 12, 1886, and Jan. 1, 1887, as quoted in Turner, *George W. Cable*, p. 203.
61. *Ibid.*
62. W. J. Cash, *The Mind of the South* (New York, 1941), pp. 93–94.
63. Woodward, *Strange Career of Jim Crow*, pp. 49–65.

If white supremacists in the other southern states enacted Jim Crow legislation to avert the possibility of future black aspirations, Louisiana segregationists did so primarily to prevent a recurrence of the epic encounter still fresh in their memories. If bigots throughout the South portrayed Jim Crow as a means of protecting the master race from degrading contact with sub-human "Sambos," such allegations in Louisiana, where men such as Pinchback, Mary, Trevigne, and Martinet had laid bare the bankruptcy of white supremacist ideology, always lacked the ring of certainty. If Louisiana whites exhibited what one historian has described as an "unusual insensitivity to human rights" after 1877,[64] it may well have been because they alone among white southerners had sampled the frightening fruits of black power before 1877.

64. Hair, *Bourbonism and Agrarian Protest*, p. 186.

Suggested Reading

The best introduction to southern race relations in the post–Civil War period remains C. Vann Woodward's classic study, *The Strange Career of Jim Crow*, 2d rev. ed. (New York, 1966), to which, since its original appearance in 1955, virtually all scholarship in this field owes a substantial debt. Thomas F. Gossett, *Race, The History of an Idea in America* (Dallas, 1963), and Claude H. Nolen, *The Negro's Image in the South: The Anatomy of White Supremacy* (Lexington, Ky., 1967), provide cogent insights into the racial attitudes and ideas of white southerners, as does Lawrence J. Friedman in *The White Savage: Racial Fantasies in the Postbellum South* (Englewood Cliffs, N.J., 1970), a brilliant study despite its penchant for capricious psychoanalytical hypotheses. Bertram W. Doyle's *The Etiquette of Race Relations in the South* (Chicago, 1937) remains a valuable study often underrated by modern scholars. Excellent interpretations of race relations in other southern states during this period are provided by Vernon Lane Wharton in *The Negro in Mississippi, 1865–1890* (Chapel Hill, 1947); George B. Tindall in *South Carolina Negroes, 1877–1900* (Columbia, S.C., 1952); Charles E. Wynes in *Race Relations in Virginia, 1870–1902* (Charlottesville, 1961); Joel Williamson in *After Slavery: The Negro in South Carolina during Reconstruction, 1861–1877* (Chapel Hill, 1965); and Lawrence D. Rice in *The Negro in Texas, 1874–1900* (Baton Rouge, 1971).

Most of the general and political histories of Louisiana during this period shed little light upon the topic of race relations. Edwin A. Davis, *Louisiana, A Narrative History*, 2d ed. (Baton Rouge, 1965); John R. Ficklen, *History of Reconstruction in Louisiana through 1868* (Baltimore, 1910); Ella Lonn, *Reconstruction in Louisiana after*

1868 (New York, 1918); and Garnie W. McGinty, *The Overthrow of Carpetbag Rule, 1876–1880* (New Orleans, 1941), provide little more than uncritical briefs on behalf of Redeemer rule and white supremacy. White Republicans are dismissed as corrupt opportunists, Louisiana Negroes as weak-minded camp followers, and the civil rights controversy as a political charade. Two conspicuous exceptions must be noted. Roger W. Shugg's *Origins of Class Struggle in Louisiana: A Social History of White Farmers and Laborers during Slavery and After, 1840–1875* (Baton Rouge, 1939) provides valuable insights into Louisiana life in the midnineteenth century. William Ivy Hair's *Bourbonism and Agrarian Protest: Louisiana Politics, 1877–1900* (Baton Rouge, 1969) offers an excellent analysis of Bourbon attitudes and political policies toward Negroes, demonstrating clearly the great disparity between the high-sounding nobility of their racial rhetoric and the narrow meanness of their racial practices.

Several studies of a more specific nature are quite helpful to the student of Louisiana race relations. A judicious examination of antebellum slavery is provided by Joe Gray Taylor in *Negro Slavery in Louisiana* (Baton Rouge, 1963). T. Harry Williams, "The Louisiana Unification Movement of 1873," *Journal of Southern History*, XI (August, 1945), offers a splendid account of that intriguing experiment in biracial politics. Germaine A. Reed, "Race Legislation in Louisiana, 1864–1920," *Louisiana History*, VI (Fall, 1965), provides a convenient summary of state laws pertaining to the race question, the most infamous of which is subjected to a detailed examination by Otto H. Olsen (ed.) in *The Thin Disguise: The Turning Point in Negro History, Plessy v. Ferguson* (New York, 1968). The study of Henry C. Dethloff and Robert R. Jones, "Race Relations in Louisiana, 1877–1898," *Louisiana History*, IX (Fall, 1968), offers many cogent observations on its topic despite its dogmatic insistence that C. Vann Woodward's hypotheses be accepted as holy writ. Howard Ashley White's *The Freedmen's Bureau in Louisiana* (Baton Rouge, 1970) is of value in spite of its preoccupation with administrative details. Betty Porter's "The History of Negro Education in Louisiana," *Louisiana Historical Quarterly*, XXV (July, 1942), contains relevant information, a characteristic not shared by *The Story of Public Education in Louisiana* (New Orleans, 1924) by Thomas H. Harris. A sprightly account of the effects of the segregation controversy on the state seminary can be found in Walter L. Fleming's *Louisiana State University, 1860–1896* (Baton Rouge, 1936). Charles B. Roussevé's *The Negro in Louisiana: Aspects of His Culture and His Literature* (New Orleans, 1937) remains the only attempt at a general history of Louisiana Negroes, an undertaking which has been shamefully neglected by more competent scholars.

There is no shortage of worthwhile studies on race relations in New Orleans. General accounts containing relevant material and invaluable background information include those by Joseph G. Tregle, Jr., in "Early New Orleans Society: A Reappraisal," *Journal of Southern History*, XVIII (February, 1952); Robert C. Reinders in *End of an Era: New Orleans, 1850–1860* (New Orleans, 1964); Gerald M. Capers in *Occupied City: New Orleans under the Federals, 1862–1865* (Lexington, Ky., 1965); and Joy J. Jackson in *New Orleans in the Gilded Age: Politics and Urban Progress, 1880–1896* (Baton Rouge, 1969). Three studies of various aspects of the city's social history should not be overlooked. Despite its lack of documentation and its annoying attempt to titillate as well as inform, Herbert Asbury's *The French Quarter: An Informal History of the New Orleans Underworld* (Garden City, 1938) offers valuable insights into the racial priorities of the city's sinners. Henry A. Kmen's *Music in New Orleans: The Formative Years, 1791–1841* (Baton Rouge, 1966) provides a detailed analysis of racial arrangements and the role of black musicians in early nineteenth-century New Orleans music, a task performed admirably for the realm of athletics in a subsequent period by Dale A. Somers in *The Rise of Sports in New Orleans, 1850–1900* (Baton Rouge, 1972).

Many excellent works have been written specifically on Negroes and different aspects of race relations in New Orleans. Antebellum slavery in the city is subjected to perceptive analyses by Robert C. Reinders in "Slavery in New Orleans in the Decade before the Civil War," *Mid-America*, XLIV (October, 1962), and Richard C. Wade in *Slavery in the Cities: The South 1820–1860* (New York, 1964). The definitive source on the city's pre–Civil War free Negro community remains Donald E. Everett's "Free Persons of Color in New Orleans, 1803–1865" (Ph.D. dissertation, Tulane University, 1952), a rambling but thorough study which certainly merits publication. My own "Racial Segregation in Ante Bellum New Orleans," *American Historical Review*, LXXIV (February, 1969), traces the development of the color line in the city up to 1861. John W. Blassingame's *Black New Orleans, 1860–1880* (Chicago), not yet published as this is written, is certain to be a valuable addition to the literature on the subject. For accounts of two post–Civil War outbreaks of racial violence with dramatically different results, see Donald E. Reynolds's "The New Orleans Riot of 1866, Reconsidered," *Louisiana History*, V (Winter, 1964), and my own "A Pioneer Protest: The New Orleans Street-Car Controversy of 1867," *Journal of Negro History*, LIII (July, 1968). Louis R. Harlan's "Desegregation in New Orleans Public Schools during Reconstruction," *American Historical Review*, LXVII (April, 1962), provides a perceptive, lucid analysis of the most controversial of all assaults upon segregation during the period.

A number of travelers through Louisiana recorded their observations and opinions on the nature of race relations in the state. Antebellum accounts include Sir Charles Lyell's *A Second Visit to the United States of North America*, 2 vols. (New York, 1849); Thomas Low Nichols's *Forty Years of American Life, 1821–1861* (New York, 1937); Ferencz and Theresa Pulszky's *White, Red, Black Sketches of American Society in the United States during the Visit of Their Guests*, 2 vols. (New York, 1853); and two of Frederick Law Olmsted's three classic narratives, *A Journey through the Seaboard Slave States*, 2 vols. (New York, 1856), and *The Cotton Kingdom*, 2 vols. (New York, 1861). Among the more pertinent post–Civil War accounts, *After the War: A Southern Tour, May 1, 1865, to May 1, 1866* (New York, 1866), by Whitelaw Reid, is in a class by itself, but Robert Somers's *The Southern States since the War, 1870–1871* (London, 1871) and John T. Trowbridge's *A Picture of the Desolated States and the Work of Restoration, 1865–1868* (Hartford, 1868) are also of value.

Unfortunately, this great profusion of narratives by visitors was not matched by native or adopted sons of Louisiana. Of all the central figures in the controversy over civil rights, only Henry C. Warmoth produced an autobiography. *War, Politics and Reconstruction: Stormy Days in Louisiana* (New York, 1930), published more than fifty years after Warmoth's retirement from politics, tells us more of an old man's pathetic desire to be accepted by white Louisiana society than it does of the factual course of events during his governorship. More helpful is Gilbert L. Dupre's *Political Reminiscences, 1876–1902* (Opelousas, La., 1918), the refreshingly candid memoir of a Democrat from St. Landry Parish who occupied a seat in the legislature during the enactment of the first "separate but equal" laws. The writings of George W. Cable on the race question are laced with autobiographic sketches and anecdotes, especially the poignant essay "My Politics," included by Arlin Turner (ed.) in *The Negro Question: A Selection of Writings on Civil Rights in the South by George W. Cable* (New York, 1958). For a harrowing account of slave life in the Red River region, see Solomon Northup's *Twelve Years a Slave* (Auburn, N.Y., 1853). No Louisiana Negroes prominent in the post–Civil War era produced memoirs.

The selection of pertinent biographical material is even more disappointing. Arlin Turner's *George W. Cable: A Biography* (Durham, 1956) remains the only adequate study of its type on a key participant in the postbellum segregation struggle. Francis B. Harris's "Henry Clay Warmoth, Reconstruction Governor of Louisiana," *Louisiana Historical Quarterly*, XXX (April, 1947), evades an examination of Warmoth's racial ideology, an oversight corrected somewhat by Richard N. Current's *Three Carpetbag Governors* (Baton Rouge, 1967). John E. Gonzales's "William Pitt Kellogg, Reconstruction Governor of Louisiana, 1873–1877," *Louisiana Historical Quarterly*, XXIX (April, 1946), sheds little upon Kellogg's commitment to civil rights. Thomas Conway, certainly the most important of the white Radical integrationists, has been ignored altogether by scholars. White supremacist leaders have fared even worse than Republicans. Alone among the South's leading Redeemers, Francis T. Nicholls has not been the subject of a published biography, though Clarence Howard Nichols's "Francis T. Nicholls, Bourbon Democrat" (M.A. thesis, Louisiana State University, 1959) at least provides a point of departure. Howard Turner's "Robert Mills Lusher, Louisiana Educator" (Ph.D. dissertation, Louisiana State University, 1944) is a mediocre study of that powerful bigot. Governors Louis Wiltz and Samuel D. McEnery, White League leader Frederick Ogden, and publisher Henry J. Hearsey are among the influential segregationists untouched by biographers. Black leaders have been ignored in similar fashion. Agnes Smith Grosz, in "The Political Career of Pickney Benton Stewart Pinchback," *Louisiana Historical Quarterly*, XXVII (April, 1944), does little to alleviate the need for a truly thorough biography of the most remarkable black politico in Louisiana history. Among the prominent black civil rights leaders yet undiscovered by biographers are Aristide Mary, Paul Trevigne, and the brothers J. B. and Louis Roudanez.

Index